Girls

Who Rocked the World

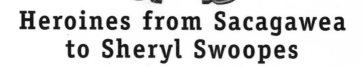

Heroines from Sacagawea to Sheryl Swoopes

By Amelie Welden

Illustrations by Jerry McCann

BEYOND
WORDS
Publishing
INC

Beyond Words Publishing, Inc.
20827 N.W. Cornell Road, Suite 500
Hillsboro, Oregon 97124-9808
503-531-8700 / 1-800-284-9673

Editors: Michelle Roehm, Mary McMahon, and Marianne Monson-Burton
Designer: Marci Doane Roth
Proofreader: Marvin Moore

Distributed to the book trade by Publishers Group West
Printed in the United States of America

Library of Congress Cataloging-in-Publication Data

Welden, Amelie, 1975—
    Girls who rocked the world : heroines from Sacagawea to Sheryl
Swoopes / by Amelie Welden.
        p.   cm.
    Includes bibliographical references.
    Summary: Tells the stories of thirty-three girls who were younger
than twenty years of age when they changed the history of the world
through amazing accomplishments.
    ISBN 1-885223-68-4
    1. Girls—Biography—Juvenile literature. 2. Women heroes—
Biography—Juvenile literature. 3. Heroes—Biography—Juvenile literature.
[1. Girls. 2. Women heroes. 3. Heroes. 4. Women—Biography.
5. Youth's writings.] I. Title.
CT3207.W45 1998
920.72—dc21   97-46043
                                                     CIP
                                                     AC

Every effort has been made to contact the copyright owners of the photographs in this book. If the copyright holder of a photograph in this book has not heard from us, please contact Beyond Words Publishing. The publisher gratefully acknowledges and thanks the following for generous assistance and permission to use photos:

Sacagawea: Bronze statue by Alice Cooper, 1905
Queen Victoria: Her Most Gracious Majesty the Queen. Mezzotint of Queen Victoria by Henry Cousins after
                George Hayter. © Museum of London
Helen Keller: American Foundation for the Blind, Helen Keller Archives
Iréne Joliot-Curie: Association Curie et Joliot-Curie
Babe Didrikson: © U.S. Olympic Committee
Anne Frank: © AFF/AFS, Amsterdam, The Netherlands
Wilma Rudolph: © U.S. Olympic Committee
S. E. Hinton: Puffin Books
Nadia Comaneci: © International Gymnast Magazine
Sheryl Swoopes: © Bill Baptiste, NBA photos
Wang Yani: Scholastic, Inc.
Vanessa-Mae Nicholson: Vanessa-Mae Nicholson
Cristen Powell: Photo by Vince Bucci © Reebok
Martina Hingis: © David Goodman

Contents

Note from the Author

1975– ✳ WRITER ✳ UNITED STATES

We stand at the beginning of a new epoch in the history of humankind's thought, as we recognize that . . . woman, like man, makes and defines history.
— Gerda Lerner, Professor of History, University of Wisconsin

What if I asked you to name some important people from history — who would you list? If you're like most of us, you'd probably name more men than women. (If not, good for you!) But why do most people think of men when they consider influential people in history? Is it because women weren't important? No way! Women's strength, ingenuity, and perseverance have always been vital in defining the world's cultures and civilizations. It's just that many stories of women and girls have been left out of traditional "history" that gets recorded and taught.

Luckily, in recent years, progress has been made toward restoring women's roles in history. While our current history books are giving more credit to women from the past, it is equally important that you, today's girls, know that you can make your own impact on the history books of tomorrow.

With these issues in mind, I set to work on *Girls Who Rocked the World*.

I am proud to be a part of retelling the history of many amazing girls and hope that my work encourages you to believe in your dreams and in your power to make a difference. By no means is this contribution mine alone; many creative and inspiring people helped along the way. I'd especially like to thank Bob Erickson, Jean Ward, and Patti Littlehales for their help in my research. Also, an outstanding group of women at Beyond Words Publishing were invaluable in all stages of the writing process. A huge "thank you" to Michelle Roehm, Mary McMahon, and Marianne Monson-Burton.

One of the most difficult parts of writing this book was choosing which girls to include. I had to make many tough choices and wanted to represent as many times, places, and pursuits as possible. There were two main qualifications a girl had to meet in order to be considered for the book: (1) She had to have achieved something extraordinary while under the age of twenty, and (2) there had to be recorded information about the girl and her life.

The age qualification made it impossible to include thousands of influential *women* whose achievements came later in life — incredible women like Sojourner Truth, an African-American slave who was a leader in the anti-slavery and women's rights movements; and Valentina Tereshkova, a Soviet astronaut who was the first woman in space. This was especially limiting in the sciences, since many women first had to complete years of study before making contributions to their fields.

The second criterion of availability of information was more complicated. Many girls' stories weren't recorded by historians at all. Also, as we go back in time, we find that most girls who were lucky enough to see their stories recorded were royalty or from the highest class. You'll read about several queens and girls who were born into positions of power in *Girls Who Rocked the World*, but keep in mind that today's situation is different. No matter what your background, every girl now has the opportunity to make a mark on the world and to be remembered for it.

As you read the following pages, remember that the girls in this book are just a few of the millions of girls who have done and will do amazing things. I hope their lives will inspire you as they have inspired me. They are definite proof that girls like you and me can achieve our goals, pursue our passions, and live our dreams. So now it's your turn to go out there and "rock the world"! After all, in the words of famous girl speaker Anna Dickinson, "The world belongs to those who take it."

Cleopatra VII

69–30 B.C. ✤ RULER OF EGYPT ✤ EGYPT

Her form, coupled with the persua-siveness of her conversation, and delightful style of behavior — all those produced a blend of magic.
— Greek historian Plutarch, speaking of Cleopatra

A small boat entered the harbor in the pitch black of night. As Cleopatra looked out over the water, she could see that the palace was surrounded by her brother's soldiers. She hoped the darkness would hide her arrival. If she was caught, she knew she would be killed on the spot. Cleopatra prayed that her plan would work. Somehow she *had* to get inside that palace.

Julius Caesar sat inside the palace, wondering how he could help Egypt settle its current difficulties. There was a knock on the door and a man came in with a carpet. Caesar watched in amazement as the leather strap was untied and the carpet was rolled out onto the floor. Out of it emerged a most striking and noble young woman. She dusted herself off and smiled at Caesar. He was mesmerized. It was the young Cleopatra, queen of Egypt, who had hidden herself in the carpet in order to meet the Roman general.

Though Cleopatra had been Egypt's queen since she was eighteen, she had recently been banished from her country by her enemies. She needed Caesar's help.

Cleopatra's life of adventure and intrigue began in 69 B.C., when she was born into the ruling family of Egypt. She was just eighteen years old at the time of her father's death, when she became the queen of Egypt. Following royal Egyptian custom, Cleopatra married her ten-year-old brother, Ptolemy XIII. They ruled Egypt jointly.

Since King Ptolemy was very young, his advisors thought they would be able to rule Egypt behind his back. But Cleopatra had her own ideas. She dreamed of restoring Egypt to the cultural and political power it had been in earlier times. She was sure she could do this, if she had the opportunity. But Ptolemy's advisors were threatened by Cleopatra's ideas and independence, and they forced her out of Egypt by the time she was twenty.

In exile, Cleopatra organized her own army to fight back. When she heard that the mighty Roman general Julius Caesar was traveling to Egypt, she devised a brilliant plan. Hidden in the carpet roll, Cleopatra snuck into Alexandria, the capital of Egypt, past her enemies, and into the palace to meet with the most powerful man in the world. She urged Caesar to help her take back her homeland from her enemies.

The brave young queen so impressed Caesar that he agreed to help her regain control of Egypt. They tried persuading Ptolemy to settle peacefully, but he refused and they were soon at war. Together, Cleopatra and Caesar defeated Ptolemy and his supporters. The fifteen-year-old king, dressed in heavy golden armor, drowned in the Nile while trying to escape his sister.

Cleopatra was crowned queen of Egypt once again, and this time she was required to marry her youngest brother, Ptolemy XIV, and make him co-ruler. But Cleopatra and Caesar had fallen in love, and she went back with him to Rome. There they shared an extravagant villa and had a son, Caesarion. Caesar's obvious love for the Egyptian queen upset Roman leaders, as they believed that Caesar wanted to make himself king of the Roman republic with Cleopatra as his queen. Plus, he already had a wife! When Caesar commissioned a golden statue of Cleopatra honoring her as a goddess and displayed it in Rome, the Romans had had enough. In 44 B.C., Caesar was murdered by members of his Senate, many of whom were his own friends.

Afraid for her life, Cleopatra and her son returned to Egypt. She was so determined to have power over the fate of her country that she had her younger brother poisoned. She then named Caesarion as her co-ruler, and for the next few years they worked hard to increase Egypt's prosperity.

Meanwhile, Marc Antony had become a powerful leader in Rome. Like Caesar, he traveled to Egypt looking for support in foreign wars. Antony and Cleopatra met, and it was not long before they too fell in love. They lived together in Egypt, where they had three children. Antony controlled much of the Roman Empire at that time, and he named Cleopatra and Caesarion as joint rulers of several Roman provinces. They were given the titles Queen of Kings and King of Kings. He also gave Roman lands to his three young children to rule. With this new land and power, Cleopatra had at last achieved her girlhood dream for Egypt.

When Marc Antony first met Cleopatra, she came sailing up the river in style. Her luxurious barge had purple sails and was filled with gold and jewels. Her servants rowed the barge with silver oars, while others played flutes and stood fanning her.

Roman leaders, especially the powerful Octavian, were shocked that Antony was giving Cleopatra so much control. Octavian declared war on Cleopatra, and at the Battle of Actium in 31 B.C., he defeated their fleet of ships. Cleopatra and Antony rushed back to Egypt to defend their kingdom on land. When Octavian attacked Alexandria, Antony was told that Cleopatra had died during the battle. He was so distraught that he threw himself on his sword and killed himself. But Cleopatra was actually still alive. She had gone into hiding in the tomb she had built in Alexandria.

Cleopatra knew that if Octavian captured her he would love to take her back to Rome as proof of his victory over Egypt. She envisioned being led through the streets of Rome in chains while the crowds ridiculed and cursed her. She would never let that happen. Instead, Cleopatra killed herself with the bite of a poisonous snake called an asp. After her death, Octavian made Egypt a part of the Roman Empire, thus giving Cleopatra her place in history as the last Egyptian Pharaoh.

In Egyptian myth, the asp was a symbol of royalty and its bite was believed to make the victim immortal.

Cleopatra led an extraordinary life that captured the imaginations of many. She has been denounced as a power-hungry tyrant and glamorized as an entrancing seductress. While most historians agree that Cleopatra was indeed beautiful, they believe her real power came from her courage, intelligence, and charisma. The Greek historian Plutarch wrote:

> [H]er beauty . . . was in itself not altogether incomparable . . . but convers[ation] with her had an irresistible charm, and her presence, combined with the persuasiveness of her discourse . . . had something stimulating about it. There was sweetness also in the tones of her voice; and her tongue, like an instrument of many strings, she could readily turn to whatever language she pleased.... [I]t is said that she knew the speech of many other peoples also, although the kings of Egypt before her had not even made an effort to learn the native language.[1]

No matter whose interpretation you believe, it is certain that Cleopatra was one of the most influential women in history. She was a clever and courageous ruler who had the mighty Roman Empire quaking in their sandals. W. W. Tarn sums up their feelings:

> Rome, who had never condescended to fear any nation or people, did, in her time fear two human beings; one was Hannibal, and the other was a woman.[2]

How Will You Rock the World?

"I'm going to rock the world by being the president of the U.S. and my husband will be the 'First Man.' Then I'll be *real* famous and everyone will read the books I write."

Brianna Headland, age 10

Joan of Arc

*I was admonished
to adopt feminine
clothes; I refused,
and still refuse.
As for other avoca-
tions of women,
there are plenty
of other women to
perform them.*

— Joan of Arc

Arrow and crossbow in hand, young Joan of Arc stood on the fortress tower and looked down into the enemy camp. This courageous, seventeen-year-old girl was about to lead the French army into war. She had already won a difficult battle, but she now focused on her final goal: to drive the English army out of the French city of Orléans. Joan's heart pounded with fear as she shot a special arrow down into the English camp. Attached to the arrow was a message telling her enemies to surrender the city or she would attack.

The English refused, and Joan once again prepared her troops for battle.

The next morning she led an assault against their army. Joan was wounded in the shoulder during the bloody battle, but in the end, Joan and her men were triumphant. On May 8, 1429, the French army regained control of Orléans due to Joan's brave, inspirational leadership.

But her mission wasn't over yet. Joan's courage and ambition would do even more to help the French. This young girl would be remembered around the world as a heroic and valiant warrior.

Joan was born on a cold January morning in the French village of Domrémy, where her father worked as a farmer. She was a deeply spiritual girl, and she had a vision of herself becoming something very different from a traditional peasant woman of that time.

During Joan's childhood, her country was in the midst of the Hundred Years' War with England. The English army invaded and took control of much of France, including Paris. Meanwhile, the king of France, Charles VI, was killed in 1422, and Rheims, the town where all French kings were traditionally crowned, was captured by the English. France went into a state of anarchy, because the "dauphin" (the oldest son of King Charles VI), could not be taken to Rheims to be crowned king.

When she was about thirteen, Joan believed she heard the voice of God telling her that she'd been chosen to accomplish great things. Over the next few years, she had visions of St. Michael, St. Catherine, and St. Margaret, who told her it was her fate to free the city of Orléans (which was on the way to Rheims) and to take the dauphin to be crowned king at Rheims — it was to be a most dangerous mission.

> The children in the village knew all about the war going on around them. Joan and her friends some-times played in an abandoned castle, pretending to be soldiers in the war.
>
>

Joan set off to meet her destiny in 1429. As a seventeen-year-old peasant girl, it was quite difficult for young Joan to convince people to help her. But she was an incredibly strong-willed girl with a persuasive personality. To begin her journey, she convinced the captain of the dauphin's forces to furnish her with a horse and a few escorts. Dressed in men's clothing, Joan traveled across war-torn France to meet the future king.

When Joan arrived, the dauphin was skeptical about the young girl's divine mission and military plan, so he summoned a group of clergy and biblical scholars to examine her. Joan conquered their disbelief and was granted her own troops to command in an attack on Orléans. She was even given the rank of captain.

The young leader armed herself for battle. She wore a suit of light armor and carried a unique sword with five crosses etched on its blade. She also carried a silk-edged white banner, decorated with an embroidered pattern of Jesus Christ holding the globe in his hands. With her new army behind her, Joan set out for Orléans.

She led a series of successful attacks against the English. Joan's fearless, inspirational leadership gave her troops the spirit and morale they needed to beat the English army in the battle. She is described as "most expert in war, as much as in carrying the lance as in mustering a force and ordering the ranks, and in laying the guns." The English were defeated and the first part of Joan's vision had come true.

After her victory in Orléans, which most French people viewed as a miracle, Joan proceeded to the next part of her vision — to take the dauphin to Rheims to be crowned. Once again she had to use her powers of persuasion to convince the dauphin of her plan. Joan set off for Rheims, defeating the English in many battles along the way and freeing all the French towns between Orléans and Rheims. The dauphin followed a week later, when he was sure it was safe. He was crowned Charles VII, King of France, in Rheims, uniting war-torn France under one leader. Joan stood at his side during the entire coronation.

In 1430, Joan tried to protect France from yet another threat: an attack by the Burgundians. She fought bravely but was captured. The Burgundians sold her to the still bitter English. They were anxious to take revenge on their female foe. The English brought Joan to trial, accusing her of witchcraft and dressing as a man (which was considered a crime against the church). The English were afraid of Joan's power and influence over the people of France, so they sentenced her to death without a fair trial.

On May 30, 1431, nineteen-year-old Joan of Arc was burned at the stake as an eager crowd watched on. The executioner said afterward, "I greatly fear that I am damned for I have burnt a holy woman."

Charles VII made no effort to save France's brave warrior, and many believe this was because he was embarrassed that France's victory was won by a peasant girl. Twenty years after Joan's death, Charles VII ordered an investigation of her trial, and the original verdict was annulled. It took almost 500 years, but finally in 1920 Joan was declared a saint by the Roman Catholic Church.

Joan of Arc's fearless leadership had a substantial influence on the Hundred Years' War. Her military victories demoralized the English and brought new hope to the people of France. Joan's life has inspired countless artists, writers, musicians, and historians. She is the patron saint of France, where her feast day, May 30, is celebrated as a national holiday. Though Joan of Arc lived for only nineteen years, her legacy of heroism has survived for centuries.

How Will You Rock the World?

"My goal is to be an astronaut and explore the universe. People who have been in the military have a better chance of being accepted into NASA, so I plan to be a naval aviator, flying F-14 Tomcats, after graduating from Annapolis. I already made it through boot camp and am a cadet in the U.S. Naval Sea Cadet Corp. I am also taking flying lessons."

Janel Hansen, age 14

"I will rock the world by becoming president of the U.S.A., and my campaign promise is to make this a hunger-free country."

Nancy Ayón, age 12

Sor Juana Inés de la Cruz

1651–1695 ❁ *SCHOLAR AND POET* ❁ *MEXICO*

Fifteen-year-old Juana nervously clamped her hands together as she looked around the room filled with forty of the most intelligent, educated men in Mexico City. She felt like she'd been answering their questions forever. But still they weren't finished with the exam. The men continued calmly interrogating her, one after another—they asked questions about philosophy, math, history, poetry, religion, and anything else they could think of. For hours she answered their questions. Would she be able to prove her extraordinary intelligence so they would allow her to continue her studies?

Over several hours, she astounded them with her brilliant answers. The stories about her were true after all. Juana's success at the exam was just the beginning of her accomplishments. She later became one of Mexico's foremost intellectuals and also one of its greatest poets!

On November 12, 1651, Juana Ramirez de Asbaje was born in a small hacienda (ranch) in a Mexican village. At the age of three, Juana began following her sister to school and quickly learned to read. She was soon able to read better than her mother. Juana's amazing intellect could not be held back, and she studied anything she could get her hands on, including math, philosophy, religion, literature, history, and the Aztec language. Amazingly, she also learned Latin, a very difficult language, on her own after taking just a few lessons.

Although Juana was a better reader than her mother, she kept it a secret. She didn't want to hurt her mother's feelings, and she also hadn't gotten permission to go to classes!

When she was seven, Juana heard about the university in Mexico City. Unfortunately, like most other schools at the time, the university accepted only male students. Still, Juana begged her mother to let her dress like a boy so she could attend the school in disguise. Her mother refused, so Juana continued to study on her own from the books in her grandfather's library. She began writing at this time, and at age eight, Juana wrote a poem for a religious festival in a nearby town.

When she was nearly ten, Juana moved to Mexico City to live with her aunt and uncle. Word of her genius spread, and after a few years she was invited to stay with the viceroy (ruler) of Mexico and his wife at their palace. There she continued her studies, entertaining the court with her poetry, songs, and plays. Juana's intellect and abilities became widely repected. When she was fifteen, she faced the extensive oral examination from Mexico's leading intellectuals. She passed with flying colors.

Juana passionately desired to continue learning, but she knew that, as a girl in Mexico during the 1600s, her role was to be a wife and mother. The only way she could be a scholar was to become a nun. She entered a convent in 1669 and became Sor (Sister) Juana Inés de la Cruz.

In the convent, she enjoyed a stimulating cultural life and often entertained the highest members of society as her guests. Best of all, she was

Juana was extremely driven about her intellectual progress. She even refused to eat cheese because she had heard that it made people stupid (which isn't true, by the way).

able to pursue her studies. She studied science using the best instruments available. The Church sometimes objected to her scientific studies, though, and once she was even asked to stop experimenting for a few months. But even then, Sor Juana couldn't give up science entirely, and she found herself making scientific observations as she performed everyday activities like cooking eggs or looking at the layout of the convent.

> In her lifetime, Sor Juana put together a library that contained four thousand books — the largest library in Mexico at that time.
>
>

Sor Juana wrote poems and plays that were published in Mexico and Spain, devoting much of her writing to the discussion of women's position in society. She argued that women should be given more power and independence.

In 1695, a terrible plague swept through Mexico, and Sor Juana became ill after nursing some of the sisters in her convent. She was unable to overcome this illness and died later that year. Today, Sor Juana lives on in her words and in her example as a brilliant scholar and writer who refused to hide her intelligence or give up her dreams.

Primero Sueno (First Dream) is considered one of Sor Juana's most important poems. Its beautiful, symbolic language tells of the awakening of the mind:

> . . . *so the fantasy was calmly copying*
> *the images of everything.*
> *and the invisible brush was shaping*
> *in the mind's colors, without light*
> *yet beautiful still, the likenesses*
> *not just of all created things*
> *here in this sublunary world, but those as well*
> *that are the intellect's bright stars,*
> *and as far as in her power lay*
> *the conception of things invisible,*
> *was picturing them ingeniously in herself*
> *and displaying them to the soul.*[3]

Eliza Lucas Pinckney

I have the business of 3 plantations to transact, which requires much writing and more business and fatigue of other sorts than you can imagine. But least you should imagine it too burthensom to a girl at my early time of life . . . . I assure you I think myself happy.
—Eliza Pinckney

Eliza's father read the telegram as the family gathered silently around him. They were all nervous, and Eliza knew it couldn't be good news. With sadness in his eyes, he told them that the military had called him back to his post in Antigua. There was no choice; he would have to leave them alone at their new home in South Carolina. "But who will take care of the plantation?" asked her mother. They all knew that their mother was too sick to run the plantation without their father. The whole family stared at seventeen-year-old Eliza when she spoke up. "I can do it," she said quietly.

Eliza was true to her word and soon began her busy days running the plantation. At 5 A.M., in the pitch dark, it was time to get up. After two hours of reading, Eliza went out to the planting fields to supervise the workers. When the sun finally rose in the east, it was time for breakfast.

After that, she spent an hour on music and another hour studying. In addition to her own lessons, Eliza taught reading to her sister and several slave girls from the plantation until dinnertime. After dinner, Eliza devoted several hours to calculating the financial books for the plantations, and then she sewed until dark. Exhausted, she finally went to bed, usually sneaking in a little more time to read or write before she fell asleep.

When little Elizabeth Lucas was born on December 28, 1722, no one knew that she was destined to become one of the great agricultural inventors of history. Born in the West Indies, where her father was stationed as a British army officer, Eliza spent her early years in Antigua, before being sent to England for her education. When she was sixteen, her family moved to South Carolina, where her father had inherited a plantation on Wappoo Creek.

A year after the family arrived in America, Eliza's father received the telegram recalling him to Antigua. Her mother was in frail health, so seventeen-year-old Eliza took on the job of running the plantation and overseeing two other family properties. With only her father's letters from Antigua to help her, Eliza ran every aspect of the plantation's business. Like other southern plantations, theirs relied heavily on slave labor. Eliza supervised more than twenty slaves and all the other employees, and she still found time to care for her mother and younger sister.

Eliza's most important contribution to the business came from her experiments with crops during her teen years. Occasionally, her father sent new kinds of seeds from Antigua, and Eliza cultivated them in the South Carolina soil. After attempts with crops such as cotton, ginger, and alfalfa, Eliza received some indigo seeds.

> While their plantation used slave labor like all the others, Eliza took time out each day to teach several slave girls to read. She hoped they would become schoolmasters for the other slave children, who normally received no education.

Indigo plants are used to make blue dye for fabric and ink. Today, many dyes can be man-made, but in Eliza's time, indigo was in high demand for its unique ability to produce permanent color. English cloth-makers depended heavily on indigo and were forced to buy large quantities from France, one of the few indigo-producing countries.

In a few years, Eliza would give French indigo growers some real competition, but not before she suffered her share of setbacks. When she first planted indigo seeds in 1740, nearly the entire crop was ruined by an early frost. Eliza had wisely saved some seeds for the next year, but they yielded only 100 bushes of the precious plant. Out of this small crop, the plantation produced a modest amount of indigo.

From the West Indies, Eliza's father sent an experienced dye-maker, who agreed to help her turn the small indigo crop into finished dye. This is a delicate process, which requires accurate timing and the correct measurement of additives. The dye-maker was afraid that if indigo succeeded in South Carolina it would compete with West Indian indigo, so he deliberately ruined Eliza's tiny crop. He added too much lime to the mix and spoiled the color.

Still determined to make her venture a success, Eliza kept planting indigo seeds. Finally, in 1744, the Wappoo plantation produced a promising crop. Eliza made seventeen pounds of indigo, six of which she shipped to England. The English cloth-makers declared her product to be as good as, and even slightly better than, the French indigo they had been using.

Delighted with her success, Eliza shared indigo seeds and taught other plantation owners in South Carolina how to grow it. Soon the new plant was flourishing all over the state; South Carolina had found a profitable new crop for export. In 1747, South Carolina plantations shipped out over 135,000 pounds of indigo, and eventually they exported more than a million pounds annually.

By the age of twenty-one, Eliza's experimental enterprise made her a rich and independent woman. She had already turned down two marriage proposals, but in 1744, she decided to marry Charles Pinckney, a prominent lawyer. They built a mansion in Charleston, but Eliza continued to supervise her family's plantations and pursue her own interests in agriculture and gardening. She experimented with various crops, including flax and hemp. Eliza even tried raising silkworms and producing silk.

Over the course of her marriage, Eliza gave birth to four children. This agricultural pioneer lived to a relatively old age, surviving through the Revolutionary War and the creation of the United States. In 1793, at the age of seventy, Eliza died of cancer. At the time of her death, Eliza's contributions to the American economy were well-known and respected. Her foresight and persistence gave South Carolina a vitally important crop, one which would help support the state's plantations for decades. At her death, President George Washington personally requested that he serve as a pall-bearer in Eliza's funeral.

Phillis Wheatley

1753–1784   🌿   POET   🌿   AFRICA AND AMERICA

Phillis Wheatley not only belongs squarely in the Black American literary tradition; she, almost single-handedly, succeeded in creating that tradition. — William H. Robinson, Professor of Black American Literature, Brown University

The terrified young African girl stood on the platform, shivering in front of the white crowd. She had hardly any clothes on and her bare feet ached in the cold Boston air. She fiddled with her front baby teeth, which were loose, as she longed for her warm home in Africa. Alone in the world since she was kidnapped from her family, she looked out at the white faces and wondered sadly whose home she would be going to now. This seven-year-old girl was about to be sold into slavery.

At that time, many families in the American colonies owned slaves to do housework and other tasks. On that gloomy day in Boston in 1761, Susannah Wheatley set out to buy a slave for her household. Susannah was searching for someone who would be a companion for her, someone who would help fill the void when her own daughter married and left home.

Among the many captured Africans standing before her, Susannah noticed the young, fragile, barefoot girl. She brought the child home, hoping she would work hard at her chores and be someone to talk with. But this young slave was destined for greater things. She was extraordinarily bright and talented, and she would overcome incredible odds to become an internationally famous poet.

Like most African slaves, not much is known about Phillis's origins. She was probably born in 1753 and was likely from the Fula tribe in western Africa. At the time, slave traders kidnapped African children and brought them to America for sale. Phillis arrived in Boston in 1761 after a long and treacherous voyage across the Atlantic aboard a "slave ship." When the Wheatleys purchased her, they gave her the name "Phillis," and according to custom, she took their last name as her own.

Phillis kept a pen and ink near her bed, and the Wheatleys let her keep a fire burning all night during the winter so she would have a warm room and be ready to write, should inspiration strike.

Phillis shocked everyone with her incredible intelligence. She was able to read English in just sixteen months, and by the age of twelve, she began to study Latin. Phillis loved to read, but her passion was poetry. When she was just fourteen years old, Phillis started to write her own poems.

Luckily, the Wheatleys were supportive of Phillis's creativity. Many slaves were treated harshly, but Phillis was encouraged to skip housework so she could read and write.

As a teenager, Phillis became a celebrity in Boston because of her poetry. She often visited prominent families and held her own in conversations with the most educated people of the city. Phillis definitely enjoyed special privileges, but the fact remained that she was a slave. She still had to deal with the overwhelming racial injustice of the time.

When she dined with white families, Phillis had to eat alone at a separate table.

When Phillis was seventeen, she wrote a poem that would bring her world recognition and fame. The poem was for a minister who had recently died, and it was published throughout the American colonies and later in London as well. Two years later a book of Phillis's poetry was published in London, and Phillis traveled to England for the first time. Phillis was the first African-American woman to be published. She was also the first

African-American author, male or female, to have book of poetry published.

When the American Revolution began in 1774, Phillis wrote a poem to honor George Washington, the commander of the American army who would soon become the president of the United States. Her poem ends:

> *Proceed, great chief, with virtue on thy side,*
> *Thy ev'ry action let the goddess guide.*
> *A crown, a mansion, and a throne that shine,*
> *With gold unfading, WASHINGTON! be thine.*[4]

Washington was very impressed with the poem and invited Phillis, to visit him at his headquarters in Cambridge. Just imagine how nervous the young Phillis must have been! But Phillis swallowed her fear again and visited America's most famous leader. By all accounts, she was a hit!

Susannah, who had become a good friend to Phillis, died that same year. But it wasn't until 1778, when John Wheatley died, that Phillis finally became a free woman. Despite the fact that much of Phillis's life was spent as a slave, her poetry often celebrated freedom. Her poems were also about Christianity, and many were elegies for famous people and personal acquaintances. Her success as a poet was remarkable, but when you think about the huge obstacles she faced as a woman, an African, and a slave in colonial America, her accomplishments become truly extraordinary.

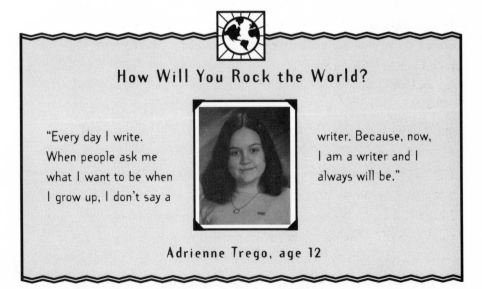

How Will You Rock the World?

"Every day I write. When people ask me what I want to be when I grow up, I don't say a writer. Because, now, I am a writer and I always will be."

Adrienne Trego, age 12

Maria Theresia Von Paradis

1759–1824 ❧ P<small>IANIST AND</small> C<small>OMPOSER</small> ❧ A<small>USTRIA</small>

Mademoiselle Paradis is the one artist whom our nation is not able to praise too highly. This gifted keyboard player is truly astonishing . . . . More faultless, more precise, more polished playing is not known.
— an anonymous reviewer of Maria's Paris concert

Maria Theresia ran her tiny fingers across the keys. She could see nothing, but she could feel their cool, smooth, comforting ivory. When she pressed down on one, out came the most clear and lovely sound. She was entranced. Although she was so young and small that she could barely reach the piano keys, Maria Theresia was drawn to the instrument.

Sure enough, this young blind girl was soon astounding audiences around the world, and she became one of the first famous woman musicians to perform in public. As a blind pianist who played, sang, composed, and taught, Maria Theresia blazed new paths not only for women but for blind people around the world.

Maria Theresia von Paradis was born in Vienna, Austria, in 1759. Her father was the royal court secretary of Empress Maria Theresa, and he named his daughter after her. When she was three years old, Maria Theresia became blind. Some believe that her blindness occurred because of an illness, while others claim she was blinded in an accident. But despite her blindness, young Maria Theresia showed an outstanding talent for music. Unable to read music with her eyes, Maria Theresia had to learn and memorize everything by ear.

She was so gifted that the empress paid for her musical and general education, and Maria Theresia was able to study music with the best teachers available. When she was eleven, she gave her first public performance, singing and playing the organ. By the time she was sixteen, Maria Theresia was recognized as a piano virtuoso and an accomplished singer.

Maria Theresia was such an amazing pianist that she inspired other great musicians — famous composers Wolfgang Amadeus Mozart and Franz Joseph Haydn both wrote piano concertos for her, and Antonio Salieri composed an organ concerto for her.

In 1783, Maria Theresia embarked on a three-year concert tour of Europe. She was highly praised wherever she went, but perhaps her most important stop was Paris. Not only did Maria Theresia play fourteen performances there, but she also met Valentin Hauy, who was planning to open the first school for the blind in Europe. Maria Theresia passionately wanted to give other blind people a chance to develop their talents in a time when people with disabilities were most often shunned by society. She described to Hauy how she had been taught math, reading, and music. He was then able to use these methods to teach the blind students in his new school.

After her tour, Maria Theresia started composing her own music. She developed a method to set down her compositions by using a peg board. Someone could then transcribe her work onto paper. The gifted musician composed at least five operas and three cantatas (compositions for voices and instruments) as well as many other shorter pieces.

One of Maria Theresia's most amazing gifts was her memory. She could play at least sixty piano concertos from memory and could remember all her own compositions, note by note.

In 1808, Maria Theresia started her own music school in Vienna; she wanted to give girls the chance for a good musical education, something that was usually reserved for boys only. Her school taught piano, singing, and music theory to both blind and sighted students.

Maria Theresia's school proved a huge success, and she continued teaching until her death in 1824. Maria Theresia worked hard to overcome not only her blindness but also the prejudice against women and people with disabilities. During her lifetime she showed the world that there are no limitations to what one girl can achieve.

How Will You Rock the World?

"I will rock the world by playing in an orchestra or band. I already play the clarinet in several bands and have played the piano at the Bronx Botanical Gardens and at Carnegie Hall three times."

Terlenda Crawford, age 12

"I'm going to rock the world by opening a school that teaches teenagers how to care for children with special needs. My classes will increase teenagers' self-confidence and respect for all disabled people, while making it easier for parents of disabled children to find qualified sitters."

Devorah Fradkin, age 14

Sacagawea

c. 1789–1812 ❋ *Guide and Interpreter* ❋ *United States*

Your woman who accompanied you that long dangerous and fatigueing rout to the Pacific Ocian and back diserved a greater reward for her attention and services on that rout than we had in our power to give her.

— William Clark, in a letter to Sacagawea's husband.

There was confusion everywhere. One of the boats was about to capsize! A few men began to bail buckets of water. Another struggled with the rudder, while two men hauled in the sail. They were all in a state of panic. In the midst of this chaos, only one member of the party stayed calm. Sixteen-year-old Sacagawea, with her newborn baby son strapped to her back, quietly balanced herself in the heaving boat.

To the horror of the entire party, some of their precious supplies spilled out into the river and began to float away. They could see food, valuable instruments—and the journals! The only records of their amazing adventure, written by their leaders, Lewis and Clark, were drifting away in the raging waters. Calm and poised, Sacagawea knew what she had to do. The men in the boat were shocked as they saw the young girl dive overboard with her baby still strapped on her back. Sacagawea rescued almost everything, including the invaluable journals.

That day, Sacagawea prevented the loss of crucial cargo, but this was just the *beginning* of the journey. The young Shoshone girl would continue to prove herself invaluable to the Lewis and Clark expedition as an interpreter, guide, and sign of peace.

Around 1789, Sacagawea was born to a Shoshone tribe in the area that is now Idaho. When she was just ten years old, she and another Shoshone girl were kidnapped by the Hidatsa Indians, who took Sacagawea hundreds of miles east to North Dakota. There she lived in a Mandan Indian village as a slave. After a few years, she was won by a French Canadian fur trader named Toussaint Charbonneau, who made Sacagawea his wife. When she was only sixteen, she gave birth to their son, whom she named Jean Baptiste but usually called "Pomp," which means "leader of men" in the Shoshone language.

In 1804, a team of explorers called the Corps of Discovery, led by Meriwether Lewis and William Clark, arrived in the Mandan villages. President Jefferson had commissioned them to explore the land west of the Mississippi, and they needed guides and an interpreter for the Native peoples they would meet. Lewis and Clark hired Charbonneau for the expedition, primarily because Lewis wanted him to bring one of his native wives to help translate for them. The sixteen-year-old Sacagawea packed up her newly born son and prepared to leave the village where she had been kept as a slave. She was heading out west, toward her homeland.

For the entire journey — thousands of grueling miles over mountains and even down water-falls — Sacagawea carried the infant Pomp in a cradleboard strapped to her back.

On the long, hard trip, Sacagawea taught the men how to find and cook edible plants so they wouldn't starve when their food supplies ran out, which happened several times. She guided the Corps through Montana and served as the interpreter with the Mandan and Shoshone tribes. Everywhere they went, Sacagawea and Pomp were a sign of peace to the native peoples of the West.

In August 1805, the explorers were desperate to find horses so they could continue their journey. They decided to try to locate Sacagawea's people, the Shoshones, for help. Sacagawea's childhood memories were all they had to guide them. Lewis wrote in his journal:

The Indian woman recognized the point of a high plain to our right which she informed us was not very distant from the summer retreat of her nation on a river beyond the mountains which runs to the west . . . she assures us that we shall either find her people on this river or on the river immediately west of its source . . . it is now all important with us to meet with those people as soon as possible.[5]

They did indeed find the Shoshones a few days later. The Shoshone chief, Cameahwait, welcomed the explorers, and in the midst of the festivities, one of the Shoshone women recognized Sacagawea. She had escaped capture on the day, years ago, when Sacagawea had been kidnapped by the Hidatsas! The two women cried and hugged each other in a very emotional reunion.

That afternoon, Lewis called a meeting between the captains of the exploration party and the chiefs of the tribe. Sacagawea was to translate to Chief Cameahwait. No sooner had they started the meeting when Sacagawea jumped to her feet and ran to embrace the chief, who had seemed so familiar to her. Chief Cameahwait was Sacagawea's brother!

The expedition party stayed as guests of the Shoshones for a month, and when they left, Chief Cameahwait gave them food, horses, and detailed instructions for their passage across the Rocky Mountains. The group successfully reached the Pacific Ocean, and the end of their exploration, in November 1805. They weathered a rainy winter in hastily built cabins before they began their return trip back to St. Louis in late March 1806.

> *Legend has it that the Nez Perce tribe planned to kill the entire Lewis and Clark expedition, but Sacagawea persuaded them that the expedition was peaceful. If they were a war party, she pointed out, they would not have taken along a girl and her baby.*

Sacagawea, Charbonneau, and Pomp started back with the expedition but went their own way before the group arrived in St. Louis. Little is know of what happened to Sacagawea after this. Some accounts say that in her early twenties she had a daughter, Lizette, and probably died in 1812, soon after the birth. Other accounts, however, claim that Sacagawea returned west to join the Shoshones and lived to be almost one hundred years old!

Sacagawea's bravery has been immortalized by numerous memorials and historical markers across America. Lakes, mountains, rivers, state parks, and even Girl Scout camps have been named after her. Sacagawea's life has become a legend of courage and adventure.

How Will You Rock the World?

"I will rock the world by embracing old age and all that it brings. Once I reach a ripe old age I will turn around to face the entire world and let tumble the oceans of knowledge I acquired in my lifetime."

Erin Wisniewski-Smith, age 16

"I'm going to rock the world by getting a degree in veterinary medicine. But instead of being a vet right away, I will first go to South America and be a mis- sionary. When I come back, I'll be a vet, breed dogs, and adopt six kids (one from every conti- nent but Antarctica, since no one but scientists live there)."

Eliza Dewey, age 9

Dr. Miranda "James" Barry

1795–1865 ❧ DOCTOR ❧ ENGLAND

Dr. James Barry, staff-surgeon to the garrison and the Governor's medical adviser . . . the most skillful of physicians. I . . . sat next to him at dinner at one of the regimental messes . . . . His style of conversation was greatly superior to that one usually heard at a mess-table in those days.
— An English general, describing Dr. Barry in 1819

T he coroner put down his instruments. His jaw dropped open and his assistants stared in disbelief. The recently deceased Dr. James Barry, a brave and distinguished man who performed surgery on worldwide battle-fields, was not a brave man after all. He was a brave . . . *woman!*

In the 1800s, women were not allowed to become doctors, but young Miranda Stuart was determined to let nothing stand in the way of her dream. As a teenager, she disguised herself as a man in order to take university classes in medicine and anatomy. She fooled everyone and became a doctor at seventeen, later becoming a successful surgeon in the English army! No one discovered her secret for over fifty years, when the autopsy betrayed her.

Nothing is known about Dr. Barry's childhood. We don't know where she came from or who her family was. Most people believe that she was born in

London in 1795 and named Miranda Stuart. Historians say she may have even been the illegitimate daughter of a noble Scottish lady and the Prince Regent of England.

The first thing we know for sure about Dr. Barry is that she graduated from the University of Edinburgh as a Doctor of Medicine in 1812, at age seventeen! The next year, Dr. Barry became an army hospital assistant. She advanced rapidly through army ranks and eventually became Inspector General, which is the highest rank possible. Dr. Barry earned the admiration of her peers, who recognized her skill, courage, and determination.

Dr. Barry's skill as a surgeon was well-known, but still she was teased for her small build, high voice, and "whisker-less" face. No one wanted a duel with Dr. Barry, however — she was an excellent shot!

During Dr. Barry's life, England had many colonies throughout the world, and Dr. Barry spent much of her time far away from her homeland. She served in Europe, Canada, South Africa, India, and Jamaica. After almost fifty years as a military surgeon, Dr. Barry retired to London in 1859.

After her death in 1865, her shocking secret was exposed. The autopsy showed not only that Dr. Barry was a woman but also that she had given birth to at least one child. When Dr. James Barry died, England mourned the loss of a highly skilled army surgeon. But no one could have dreamed that they were also mourning the loss of England's first female doctor.

How Will You Rock the World?

"Finding a cure for cancer is one out of the many ways that I'll rock the world. Today cancer is a mystery, but I'm going to solve that mystery."

Maria Ayón, age 13

Mary Anning

1799–1847 ❧ *Fossil Hunter* ❧ *England*

E leven-year-old Mary gathered her hammer and chisel and set out for the white cliffs along the Dover coast. The night before there had been a violent storm, with strong winds and droves of rain. She knew the water had washed away layers of dirt and uncovered new shells and fossils. With any luck, she'd be able to find a few unique specimens to sell at her curiosity shop.

As Mary walked along the beach, she noticed something strange. Lying near one of the cliffs were some objects that appeared to be large bones. Intrigued, she immediately went to get a closer look. Mary began chiseling away the rock near the bones, and the more she uncovered, the more excited she became. In front of her was a huge skeleton, unlike anything she'd ever seen. With its long tail, short flippers, and sharp teeth, it looked like a sea dragon!

What Mary had *really* found was one of the first and most complete skeletons of an *Ichthyosaurus*, or "fish lizard," a dinosaur that lived about 200 million years ago. This thrilling childhood discovery inspired her to spend the rest of her life hunting for fossil remains, an occupation that would bring her fame and respect in the world of science.

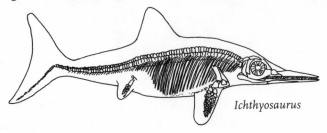

Ichthyosaurus

Mary Ann Anning was born in 1799 in Lyme Regis, a town on the southern coast of England. Her father was a carpenter who collected and sold fossils as a hobby. He often took Mary and her brother to search the coast for shells, sea dollars, and other interesting items. Tourists loved the coiled fossil shells that the Annings sold in their shop. At the time no one knew exactly what these were, but it would later be discovered that they were the fossil remains of ammonites, prehistoric mollusks that lived during the time of the dinosaurs.

When her father died in 1810, eleven-year-old Mary decided to run his curiosity shop herself. She found her first dinosaur skeleton just a few months later. She hired some quarrymen to extract it from the rock and then sold the skeleton to a man who bought things for museums. Mary's creature was later named *Ichthyosaurus*.

After this first discovery, Mary continued with her business, always searching for new fossils. When she was twenty-two, she discovered a second

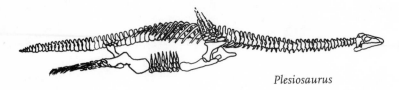

Plesiosaurus

dinosaur skeleton. This one was called a *Plesiosaurus*, or "near lizard," because of its long, thin body and its four elongated flippers that looked almost like legs. A few years later, Mary found the skeleton of a birdlike dinosaur, the first ever to be found in England, which was later named *Pterodactyl*, or "wing finger."

For the remainder of her life, Mary continued hunting and selling fossils. Mostly she sold the small fossilized shells to tourists, but her dinosaur skeletons attracted the attention of wealthier and more scholarly customers as well. Over the course of her career, she found other ichthyosaurs and plesiosaurs, which brought high prices from scientists and collectors and increased the world's knowledge about these ancient creatures.

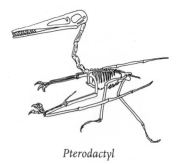

Pterodactyl

By the time she died in 1847, Mary had become well-known for her discoveries. As a prehistoric-fossil hunter, she helped found a new area of study. And as one of the earliest professional female scientists, she opened new doors for women.

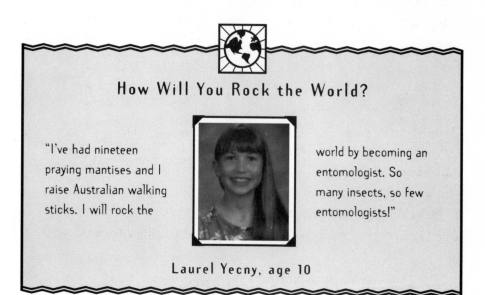

How Will You Rock the World?

"I've had nineteen praying mantises and I raise Australian walking sticks. I will rock the world by becoming an entomologist. So many insects, so few entomologists!"

Laurel Yecny, age 10

Queen Victoria

Today is my 18th birthday! How old! and yet how far am I from being what I should be. I shall from this day take the firm resolution to study with renewed assiduity . . . and to strive to become every day less trifling and more fit for what, if Heaven wills it, I'm some day to be!
— Victoria, from her diary, May 24, 1837

As she entered Westminster Abbey, nineteen-year-old Victoria could feel the eyes of a thousand people watching her. She looked both beautiful and regal in her golden dress, the first of three she would wear that day. Over it she wore a sumptuous, crimson velvet cloak bordered with gold lace and lined with fur. She could see that every detail for her coronation ceremony had been taken care of—trumpeters and cavalry greeted her coach at the entrance, the inside of the Abbey was draped with crimson cloth trimmed with gold, foot guards lined the aisles, and even the crown had been altered. A smaller, lighter crown had been made just for her, as the original one made for King George IV weighed over seven pounds!

Young Victoria felt like she'd been waiting for this day for her entire life, but actually it had been just eight years since she first learned she would one day be crowned queen of England. And now that day was here. Victoria was nervous but also excited. She knew she would be a good ruler, but few could have predicted that she would have the longest reign in English history.

Alexandrina Victoria was born in London on May 24, 1819. She was the only child of Edward, duke of Kent, and Princess Mary Louisa Victoria of Saxe-Coburg. Victoria's father died when she was only eight months old, so her mother raised her. She spent a lonely childhood in Kensington Palace, where her mother isolated her from outside influences and exerted strict control over her activities. A German tutor taught her religion, drawing, languages, and singing, but Victoria wasn't permitted to read anything except books of religion and poetry. At night, she wasn't allowed her own room but had to share one with her mother.

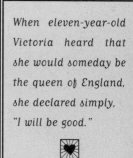

When eleven-year-old Victoria heard that she would someday be the queen of England, she declared simply, "I will be good."

When she was eleven, Victoria first learned that she would likely be crowned queen of England someday. At age eighteen, she was declared queen and was officially crowned one year later. Victoria's poise and dignity made her immediately popular with her subjects. One said, "She never ceases to be a Queen, but is always the most charming, cheerful, obliging, unaffected Queen in the world." Though she had a powerful presence and commanding voice, Queen Victoria's kind disposition was known by all. At the coronation, an old man fell as he was coming to bow before the new queen. Ignoring protocol, Victoria cried out, "May I not go and meet him?" and went down the steps to help him to his feet.

After her coronation, Victoria and her mother moved into Buckingham Palace. The new queen asserted her independence right away by assigning herself a private room on the opposite end of the palace from her mother's.

In 1840, the queen married Prince Albert of Saxe-Coburg-Gotha, and he soon came to share in his wife's political responsibilities. The two had a loving marriage and were devoted to their large family. While maintaining her royal responsibilities, Queen Victoria gave birth to nine children, all of whom were eventually married into ruling families throughout Europe.

Victoria had a grand presence, but she stood less than five feet tall.

During the 1850s, Victoria's popularity grew. In 1851, the royal family held the Crystal Palace Exhibition, a successful display of the world's techno-logical wonders. A few years later, during the Crimean War (1853-1856), the queen introduced the Victoria Cross for military bravery and supported the medical reforms pioneered by nurse Florence Nightingale.

Victoria faced the most difficult period in her life when Albert died in 1861. Devastated, the queen disappeared from public life for years. Even after she resumed her public duties, she dressed in mourning black until she died.

Victoria's seclusion hurt her popularity. Prime minister and friend Benjamin Disraeli finally persuaded her to return to the public sphere. In 1876, he pushed Parliament to transfer power over India, which was one of England's colonies at the time, to the crown. Parliament declared Victoria "Empress of India." The queen had always advocated the expansion of the British Empire, and as she was greatly honored to receive this title, with India in her empire, Queen Victoria added two million people and 800,000 square miles to the already vast British Empire!

The queen's popularity was soon restored, and her reign was celebrated in the 1887 Golden Jubilee and the 1897 Diamond Jubilee. Her death in 1901 ended Queen Victoria's sixty-four-year rule of England, the longest reign in English history. She ruled the most powerful nation in the world with stability and dignity, and she always strived to be a wise and kind leader. Her combi-nation of elegance and practicality made Queen Victoria a symbol of national unity and pride in England, and her name has even come to identify the era in which she lived: the "Victorian Age."

Virginia Reed

V irginia rubbed her frozen toes. She could no longer feel her feet inside her thin boots. She had been out with her mother and a friend in the snow for three days and three nights, with no shelter and little food. In spite of the horrible conditions, they had been able to scale the steep mountain pass that stood in the way of their escape. Thirteen-year-old Virginia was so exhausted and weak from hunger that she could only move forward by crawling on her hands and knees. Now, without any feeling in her feet, what hope was there for leaving the mountains?

She dreaded the thought of returning to camp—the dark, cold shacks, the crowded beds, the slow dying all around her, and the desperate, starving survivors. But more than that, she feared a cold death in the mountains. As the snow flew around her, she looked for her mother and wondered what would come of them. Would they ever make it to California, or would they die in this snowy prison?

Virginia Elizabeth Backenstoe was born in 1833 in Illinois — far, far away from California. Her father died when she was young, and her mother, Margaret, married James Reed, a furniture maker in Springfield, Illinois. Virginia was the oldest of the four children they raised.

In May 1846, when Virginia was thirteen, the Reed family decided to emigrate to California because of the warm weather, cheap land, and fertile soil that they expected to find there. They packed their belongings into three covered wagons and set off for the West Coast. The Reeds began their journey with friends, the Donners, and soon other pioneer families joined them. The large group became known as the Donner Party.

Days were long and difficult on the trip. Most of the group walked the entire journey, over a thousand miles, next to their wagons, struggling over hills and canyons, floating across rivers, and trekking through dry wastelands. Virginia's grandmother died early in the trip.

The trail ended in Utah, and the group made its way across the Salt Lake Desert. Many of the oxen died, the party ran low on food, and their tempers were short. Frustrated by the difficulties, Virginia's stepfather got in a fight and stabbed a man. He was banished from the group as punishment and sent alone into the desert with only a weak horse. Virginia managed to slip him some crackers and his rifle and ammunition before he left. With these supplies, he was able to survive the journey to California alone.

Meanwhile, the wagon train reached present-day Reno, at the base of the Sierra Nevada. As the wagons climbed into the mountains, a snowstorm descended on the group. Their food was nearly gone, most of their oxen and horses had died, and the snow stopped them from going any farther. They decided to make camp for the winter. For the next three months, the Donner Party lived in makeshift cabins and tents that sheltered them from the snow. They had to eat their remaining oxen and horses, and they even boiled the animal hides to produce a gluelike substance to eat.

Life in the cabins was crowded and dreary. Virginia shared her small hut with fourteen other travelers, many of whom were starving. Despite the horror of the situation, there were a few happy times in the cabin. Virginia was grateful to have family to talk with and a few books to read.

Several times, small parties tried to leave the camp and cross the mountains into California. One party of fifteen left in December, and only seven survived — five of the survivors were women. They organized a rescue party when they reached California, but it was months before they made it to the camp.

Virginia also tried to cross the mountains. In early January she tried to make the crossing with her mother, a hired helper, and a family friend. The helper turned back after just one day, but the other three went on. Although Virginia was so weak that she sometimes had to crawl on her hands and knees, they managed to scale the pass.

Virginia's favorite book was Daniel Boone, a tale she read over and over again. Perhaps his story of hard times on the frontier gave her courage and hope for her own situation.

After three days and nights out in the snow, Virginia's feet were frostbitten, and the small party had to return to camp.

By February, Virginia was very ill. Most of the pioneers were sick, and many had died from starvation. The survivors, desperate for food, ate the corpses of those who died. Luckily, Virginia never had to resort to this. A woman in her cabin had saved some scraps of dried meat, which she shared with the sick girl.

Finally, more than three months after that first snowstorm, the first group of rescuers reached the Donner camp. They decided to lead the strongest survivors to California first, including Virginia, her mother, and one of her little brothers. On their way down the mountains they met Virginia's stepfather, who had made it to California alone and was coming to get them with his own rescue party. After making sure they were all right, he and his rescue party went on to the camp to save the rest of the survivors, including the other two Reed children.

When they started across the Sierra Nevada, the Donner Party numbered eighty-seven. Only forty-seven survived the trip, and they had endured hardships almost beyond belief. Shortly after she arrived in California, young Virginia wrote about the ordeal in a long letter to her cousin back in Illinois. Here is how she described her life in the mountains:

There was 15 in the cabon we was in and half of us had to lay a bed all the time thare was 10 starved to death then we was hadly abel to walk . . . it snowed and would cover the cabin all over so we could not git out for 2 or 3 days.[6]

She also details her final journey into California:

[W]e went over great hye mountain as strait as stair steps in snow up to our knees. Litle James walk the hole way over all the mountain in snow up to his waist. He said every step he took he was a gitting nigher Pa and somthing to eat . . . when we had traveld 5 days we me[t] Pa with 13 men going to the cabins . . . you do not now how glad we was to see him . . . he heard we was coming and he made some s[w]eet cakes to give us.[7]

Virginia managed to put the terrible events behind her and start a new life. She settled with her family in San Jose, California, married in 1850, and had nine children. After surviving one of the most terrifying experiences imaginable, Virginia was happy to lead a quiet family life until she died in 1921. Virginia's courage and will enabled her to endure nearly four months of freezing weather and starvation, and her letter to her cousin survives as the most detailed firsthand account of the Donner Party tragedy.

How Will You Rock the World?

"I will rock the world by hiking the Appalachian National Scenic Trail, the mountain range which stretches from Maine to Georgia. All 2,140 miles!"

Erin Metcalf, age 12

Anna Elizabeth Dickinson

1842–1932 ✤ *ORATOR, ABOLITIONIST, AND SUFFRAGETTE* ✤

UNITED STATES

[Anna] dressed as she desired; she traveled where and how she willed; she delivered lectures on subjects many people felt should not even be mentioned in the presence of unmarried young ladies.

— Ghiraud Chester

The young speaker stood in front of more than eight hundred people. It was Anna's first full-length speech, and she was understandably nervous. Some of the people in the audience seemed to be looking at her with doubt, as if they were saying to themselves, "How could this teenage girl tell us anything we don't already know!" As she began her discussion on "The Rights and Wrongs of Women," Anna's large blue eyes scanned the audience. Her knowledge of the subject was so thorough that she needed very few notes. With each word she spoke, eighteen-year-old Anna felt more confident. The skepticism was quickly fading from the faces in the audience.

Young Anna passionately expressed her views, arguing that women should be allowed to vote and to hold any job they wanted. At the time, women in the United States were not allowed to vote or to become doctors, lawyers, or many other professions. Anna's opinions were radical for the time, but her clear voice and dramatic style impressed everyone in the audience. After two hours of speaking, Anna stepped down from the platform amid loud applause. She had just begun a career that would make her one of the most famous and influential women of her time.

Anna Elizabeth Dickinson was born on October 28, 1842, in Philadelphia, Pennsylvania. It was a time in the United States when tensions were high. Slavery was a hotly debated issue: should it be legal in all states, some states, or should it be outlawed altogether? Anna was the youngest of five children born into an abolitionist family. (Abolitionists wanted to outlaw slavery.) Anna was raised with the belief that slavery was morally wrong, and she was involved in the anti-

Anna's childhood home was actually a station on the Underground Railroad, a secret organization that helped slaves escape and become free.

slavery movement from a very young age. When she was just fourteen, she even wrote an article for an anti-slavery newspaper.

Anna attended school until she was fifteen years old, when she had to start working to help support her family. She held various jobs in publishing houses, law firms, and schools. When she was seventeen, Anna attended a meeting on women's rights. This young girl spoke up, expressing her views that women should be given the same opportunities as men. Her speaking ability was so impressive that she was soon asked to contribute to other debates on women's rights and slavery.

Anna gave her first full-length speech at the age of eighteen, and her successful career as an inspiring speaker had begun. She toured the country, gaining the respect of revolutionary leaders such as abolitionist William Lloyd Garrison and women's rights activists Susan B. Anthony and Lucretia Mott.

In 1863, Anna was asked to become a campaign speaker. She began delivering powerful

During her tours across the country, Anna enjoyed mountain climbing. She climbed many of the highest peaks in Colorado — at a time when women were considered too frail for exercise!

speeches in support of the Republican candidate for governor in New Hampshire. When the candidate won, Anna's persuasive speeches were hailed as a major reason. Her success led many politicians to invite Anna to be their campaign speaker in elections. Her fame as an orator continued to grow.

Perhaps her most important speaking engagement occurred in 1864 when Anna was formally invited to speak in front of Congress. She was the first woman ever to speak before the House of Representatives! After this speech she was introduced to President Lincoln, for whom she later campaigned when he was up for re-election.

Anna was often compared to the brave French heroine Joan of Arc, who was the subject of one of her most popular speeches.

Between her campaign speeches, Anna continued to speak out about the evils of slavery, a topic that grew more and more controversial as the nation moved toward war. During the Civil War, the United States fought over her cause, the abolition of slavery, and Anna was undoubtedly the most famous female speaker in the country. At the war's end, her powerful words were acted upon — the slaves were freed.

Anna traveled the country delivering more speeches on controversial topics. She knew that she couldn't shy away from subjects just because they weren't popular. The world needed her message. Only through open debate could these problems be solved. So Anna dared to stand up for what she believed, even when there were many who disagreed with her. Her obvious independence, courage, and passion shocked many people but earned her the respect of a great many others.

Here's an excerpt from one of Anna's speeches:

> *Give to every child in America a spelling book and a free schoolroom, and to every intelligent and respectable person, black and white, man and woman, a ballot and freedom of government, and you will see that this country will stand stronger and stronger amidst the ruins of dissolving empires and falling thrones.*[8]

Anna worked to promote racial and political equality for all. At the National Loyalists' Convention in 1866, she joined Theodore Tilton and Frederick Douglass in developing an idea for an amendment to the U.S. Constitution. The amendment would outlaw discrimination based

> Anna never married, although she had at least three offers.
>
>

on "race, sex, color, or previous condition of servitude." Their proposal was accepted by the Republicans and became the fifteenth amendment to the Constitution. Unfortunately, the word "sex" was omitted from the final amendment and inequality between men and women was not outlawed.

Anna's career paved the way for other female activists and strong women. In the 1870s, she retired from public speaking and instead began writing and acting in plays. Anna lived to be ninety years old and enjoyed success in the theater as well. But this outspoken woman will always be remembered for her fame and influence as one of the greatest speakers the United States has ever known.

How Will You Rock the World?

"I will rock the world by being the first female, Jewish president of the United States. Some of the important issues I would take charge of are comparable pay for women and better maternity leave policies."

Bassie Shusterman, age 14

Sarah Bernhardt

1844–1923 ❧ ACTRESS ❧ FRANCE

It is not at all necessary to be handsome or pretty; all that is needful is charm, the charm that holds the attention of the spectator, so that he listens rapt, and on leaving seeks to be alone, in order to recapture the charm he has felt.

— Sarah Bernhardt

The curtains pulled back and light flooded the stage. Young Sarah squinted out at the audience and could barely make out the faces of the experienced actresses and actors who had come to judge her performance. She was ready — she had practiced and practiced the scene for her entrance exam for acceptance into the prestigious French theater company. The judges stopped her. "You need to choose a boy to act in the scene with you," they said. Sarah was horrified. She had rehearsed the scene alone. She didn't even *know* any of these boys. How could she concentrate on her lines with some boy messing up her scene? "I won't," she told them.

The judges were shocked at her stubbornness but offered to let her choose another piece instead. Sarah was terrified. She hadn't practiced anything else. What scene would she do now? Then it struck her—she would tell them a story. She chose a fable she knew and began to recite it. Again, the judges were bewildered—it was a very odd choice—but after the first few lines, the panel was captured by her clear, melodious voice. Before she could even finish, she had been accepted. Fourteen-year-old Sarah had become a member of the Conservatoire of the Comédie Française. It was just the beginning of a long path that would lead her to become known as "The Divine Sarah" and the greatest actress of all time.

Sarah Bernhardt was born Rosine Bernard on October 22, 1844, in Paris. Sarah's mother was a Jewish woman from Holland who was known for her beauty and her love of travel. Sarah never knew her father. While her mother traveled around Europe, Sarah was cared for by family and friends. At twelve, she entered a convent school and a few years later decided she wanted to become a nun and teacher at the school.

Sarah was always known as a rebellious and dramatic girl. She was even suspended three times from her convent school.

Sarah's family, however, wasn't sure that she should make such an important decision when she was only fourteen years old. A family friend suggested that she study acting at the Conservatoire of the Comédie Française, a prestigious French theater. After her unusual but brilliant entrance performance, Sarah was accepted into the acting school.

Sarah studied at the Conservatoire for a few years and then performed at the Comédie Française. She made her first stage appearance when she was seventeen, but she received mixed reviews. After two more disappointing performances and a violent argument with a lead actress, Sarah left the company. She continued to act over the next few years and even tried her hand at singing, despite being tone-deaf.

Sarah didn't give up. She signed with another theater company and trained intensively for six years. Her acting received consistent good reviews, and she developed a loyal following of fans who called her "The Divine Sarah." Her big break came in 1869, when she played a page in a play called *Le Passant*, which ran for over one hundred nights in Paris. Sarah was on her way to a long-lasting and triumphant career.

Le Passant was so highly acclaimed that Napoleon himself asked for a command performance in his palace garden.

The tragedies of the next few years interrupted Sarah's path to success, however. First, a fire in her Paris apartment destroyed everything she owned. Then, the Franco-Prussian War began, and Paris was under attack. During the siege, Sarah created a hospital in the theater where she performed.

After the war ended in 1871, Sarah returned to the stage. She was praised for her role in *Ruy Blas,* which was written and directed by famous author Victor Hugo. Her energy and emotion were riveting, and she delivered her lines with entrancing poeticism. Her performance was so well-received that she was invited once again to act at the Comédie Française. There Sarah enjoyed success after success, firmly establishing her place as a leading actress.

Offstage, Sarah was known to be quite eccentric. She had many exotic pets, including a lion and a monkey. She also had a special coffin made, which she slept in.

Sarah loved to take on challenging roles. Her most controversial performance was in *L'Aiglon.* All of Paris's most prominent citizens turned out to see fifty-six-year-old Sarah portray a young man. This groundbreaking actress was one of the very first to play male roles, an idea that shocked many people. Proving the skeptics wrong, Sarah delivered a superb performance as Napoleon's illegitimate son. And when she was sixty-four years old, Sarah took on the role of one of her greatest heroines — nineteen-year-old Joan of Arc!

After achieving great fame in France, Sarah became an international star, touring Europe and North and South America. She began producing plays and even bought her own theater, which she named the Théâtrê Sarah Bernhardt. Sarah's passion for theater was unconquerable. When she was seventy-one, her leg had to be amputated due to an injury, but she refused to give up acting. Instead, she reworked all her scenes so she could remain seated throughout the plays. Sarah continued acting until she was seventy-eight years old!

After acting in hundreds of plays and earning international fame, Sarah died in Paris in 1923. The world mourned the loss of a legendary actress, who was arguably the greatest of all time. Sarah was one of the first true international celebrities in the theater. Her performances and her life were the very definition of stardom.

Sarah had many rocky love affairs. She once married an actor in her company, only to divorce him a few months later.

Emma Lazarus

1849–1887 ✤ Poet ✤ United States

Fourteen-year-old Emma sat alone in her room. She was bored with her music and language studies and thought she'd try something new. She dipped her pen in ink and began to capture on paper the words that floated in her mind. The more she wrote, the more difficult it got. She had no practice with meter or rhyme and the whole endeavor was a struggle. After hours of work and many sheets of crumpled paper, Emma was ready to give up on writing poetry. But something inside her told her to keep trying. Something wanted her to put those beautiful words on paper, so she kept going. Years later her hard work would pay off—her words of poetry were engraved into the base of the Statue of Liberty, there forever to greet the millions of immigrants who come to America.

On July 22, 1849, Emma Lazarus was born into a Jewish family in New

York City. From an early age, Emma was interested in reading and writing. In addition to common school subjects, private tutors taught her music, European literature, American poetry, and foreign languages like German, French, and Italian. Emma began writing her own poetry when she was about fourteen years old.

Emma's talent with words was so great that her first volume of poetry was published when she was just seventeen years old. She went on to write a novel, a play, and many more poems and magazine essays. She soon became a well-known, respected American author.

Emma was inspired by nature, music, and art, but she was especially moved by social issues. In the 1880s, Jews in Eastern Europe were facing horrible discrimination and persecution. As thousands of Jews immigrated to New York in order to escape, Emma became aware of their struggles. She began writing poems that dealt with Jewish persecution through history. She also wrote a play about medieval persecution of Jews, and she translated medieval Jewish poems. She collected these poems and the play into *Songs of a Semite*, which was published in 1882.

In 1886, Emma received the greatest honor of her life. Her poem "The New Colossus" was engraved on the podium of the Statue of Liberty. Her words welcome all immigrants who sail to the United States in hope of a safe haven from persecution. Today, her poetry still greets immigrants, even if they arrive in New York by airplane instead of ship. The last few lines of Emma's poem are now inscribed on the wall of the Reception Hall in the New York International Airport.

> *Emma didn't just write about the social causes she believed in — she took action. She visited the main immigration camps and helped new Jewish immigrants adapt to life in New York. She also helped found the Hebrew Technical Institute, providing much-needed education for the new immigrants.*

THE NEW COLOSSUS

Not like the brazen giant of Greek fame
With conquering limbs astride from land to land;
Here at our sea-washed, sunset gates shall stand
A mighty woman with a torch, whose flame

Is the imprisoned lightning, and her name
Mother of Exiles. From her beacon-hand
Glows world-wide welcome; her mild eyes command
The air-bridged harbor that twin cities frame,
"Keep, ancient lands, your storied pomp!" cries she
With silent lips, "Give me your tired, your poor,
Your huddled masses yearning to breathe free,
The wretched refuse of your teeming shore,
Send these, the homeless, tempest-tost to me,
I lift my lamp beside the golden door!"[9]

How Will You Rock the World?

"I will rock the world by rewriting the textbooks in 'kid language.' My goal is to have a child pick up a school book and not think of it as a chore, but as an adventure. If knowledge doesn't rock our world, I don't know what will!"

Holly Metcalf, age 14

"I will rock the world by teaching the love of learning. Imagine a future generation with the knowledge and skills to rock the world."

Tzipora Novack, age 14

Helen Keller

1880–1968 ✸ WRITER AND ADVOCATE FOR THE BLIND ✸ UNITED STATES

S ix-year-old Helen stood near the water pump and held one hand under a stream of rushing water. With her other hand, she felt the movements of her teacher's hand as Anne used sign language to spell out *w-a-t-e-r*. Blind and deaf, Helen had spent most of her childhood unable to communicate with anyone around her. Because she could not hear, she had forgotten that objects had names; she had forgotten the concept of language. But now, here at the water pump, it was all coming back to her. She finally *understood*! This coldness that she washed her hands in everyday was *water*. "What are the names for everything else?" she wondered excitedly. "What is my name?"

With Anne's help, Helen took her first step toward learning to communicate. Eventually, Anne would help Helen overcome her disabilities, teaching her to read, write, and even speak. Helen's triumph changed attitudes toward disability; she taught the world that people with disabilities may live life in a different way, but they are still able to make great contributions to society.

Helen Keller was born on June 27, 1880, in Tuscumbia, Alabama. She was a bright child who could walk and speak a few words before her first birthday. But tragedy struck when Helen became ill at nineteen months. This illness left her blind and deaf, and for the next five years, Helen lived in a dark, silent world. Like any other little girl, she had toys and liked to play. She especially liked dolls, and her favorite was one she named Nancy. But Helen had a fitful temper, and she sometimes beat her beloved doll only to hug it lovingly a few minutes later.

Such behavior worried Helen's parents, but they had no way to communicate with their child. They taught her a few easy signs, like shaking her head "yes" and "no" and pretending to cut a piece of bread to show that she was hungry. She could also perform some everyday tasks like folding and putting away clothes. But the Kellers worried that their daughter would never learn the difference between right and wrong and that they would never be able to tame her violent temper.

When Helen was six years old, the Kellers hired Anne Sullivan as her teacher. Anne, herself, was barely twenty years old when she arrived, and she had overcome her own difficulties. As a fourteen-year-old orphan, she entered the Perkins Institute for the Blind. Anne was legally blind and could not read, but she learned quickly at the school. A series of operations almost fully restored her eyesight, but her traumatic experience with blindness motivated her to help other blind children.

Now Anne faced the difficult task of teaching Helen. For the first couple of weeks, she gave Helen objects and then spelled their names into her hands. But Helen didn't associate the objects with the words until the day at the water pump. From that day forward, Helen made rapid progress. By the end of the summer she had learned 625 words. Over the next few years, she learned to read braille, to write, to type, and even to speak.

At this time, the education of people with disabilities was very controversial. Most people thought that it was not possible or worthwhile to educate disabled people, but Helen and Anne proved how ridiculous this idea was. Helen attended regular schools and devoured literature, math, history, and foreign languages. Against all the odds, twenty-year-old Helen was accepted into prestigious Radcliffe College in 1900. Anne attended classes with her, signing the lectures into her hand. Four years later, Helen graduated at the very top of her class.

> The most difficult subject for Helen was math, but she loved to read and write — and her first autobiographical story was published when she was just fourteen!

Helen devoted the rest of her life to writing and advocating the rights of the blind. Her first book, *The Story of My Life*, was published in 1903 and became a best-seller that has been translated into over fifty languages. Soon afterward, Helen and Anne embarked on a lecturing tour of the United States and Europe. Helen spoke out for women's rights and international peace. Her most important work, however, was with the American Foundation for the Blind. Helen called for better education and employment for blind people, and through her celebrity she made the public aware of the changes that were necessary. For her courageous work, she was awarded the Presidential Medal of Freedom in 1964.

Helen attributed her success to her devoted teacher, Anne. In *The Story of My Life*, Helen wrote:

> The most important day I remember in all my life is the one on which my teacher, Anne Mansfield Sullivan, came to me. I am filled with wonder when I consider the immeasurable contrasts between the two lives which it connects . . . . On the afternoon of that eventful day, I stood on the porch, dumb, expectant. I guessed vaguely from my mother's signs and from the hurrying to and fro in the house that something unusual was about to happen, so I went to the door and waited on the steps . . . . I felt approaching footsteps. I stretched out my hand as I supposed to my mother. Some one took it, and I was caught up and held close in the arms of her who had come to reveal all things to me, and, more than all things else, to love me.[10]

Helen and Anne had a close friendship and worked together until Anne's death in 1936. Together, they broke down barriers of education and discrimination, forever changing the way the world thinks of people with "disabilities."

Bessie Smith

1894–1937 ✻ *SINGER AND "EMPRESS OF THE BLUES"* ✻

UNITED STATES

Bessie used to thrill me at all times. It's the way she could phrase a note in her blues, a certain something in her voice that no other singer could get . . . she had . . . music in her soul and and felt everything she did.

— Louis Armstrong, jazz trumpet player

L ittle Bessie's throat was getting tired. She'd been singing outside the market all day long. Lots of people passed by, and many stopped to listen to the sweet voice of the nine-year-old girl dressed in her Sunday best. But not too many left money in her hat. Her stomach was growling for dinner and she couldn't wait to get home. But as she looked down at the few coins sitting in her hat, she knew it wasn't enough. With no mother or father to support them, her brothers and sisters were counting on her. She would just have to stay a little longer. A small crowd gathered as Bessie belted out a soulful tune that gave them all goosebumps. She had no idea that soon a famous singer would hear her voice. Bessie was about to be "discovered." In time, this frail young girl would become the "Empress of the Blues."

Elizabeth Smith was born on April 15, 1894, in Chattanooga, Tennessee, a bustling town of about 30,000 people. Nearly half of Chattanooga's population were African-Americans, many of whom were unemployed and extremely poor. In a time of racial discrimination and segregation, African-American families had to work hard just to scrape by. Since both of Bessie's parents died at a young age, she and her siblings earned money any way they could. Throughout her childhood Bessie spent her days singing on the streets for pocket change.

When Bessie was nine years old she made her stage debut in a local theater. She earned eight dollars for her performace. Gertrude "Ma" Rainey, one of the first blues singers ever, was in the audience and was so impressed with Bessie's powerful voice that she invited her to be in a traveling show she sang with. From then on Ma was Bessie's mentor and voice teacher. Later, when Ma formed her own group called the Rabbit Foot Minstrels, Bessie toured with this troupe as well.

Soon Bessie's music became so popular that she could perform on her own. She traveled throughout the South, playing in theaters, clubs, and meeting halls. In 1921, Bessie started performing in Northern cities, too. Her raw, powerful voice drew large crowds, and she became well-known for her dramatic style. She was often accompanied by the most talented musicians of the day, including trumpeter Louis Armstrong, pianist Fletcher Henderson, and trombonist Charlie Green.

Bessie made her first record, *Down Hearted Blues*, in 1923, and by the end of the year, it had sold over 780,000 copies. In the course of her career, she recorded more than 150 albums and sold more than ten million records. This is an

> As an African-American, Bessie often faced segregation and prejudice when she toured, but she refused to be intimi-dated. One day, when she was threatened by members of the Ku Klux Klan, Bessie scared them away, yelling "You better pick up them sheets and run!"

> "The greatest blues singer in the world will never stop singing" are the words carved on Bessie's tombstone, which was purchased by Janis Joplin and other musi-cians in 1970. Before that, Bessie's grave had been unmarked.

amazing total, since Bessie sang at a time when most people didn't even own record players!

In 1937, Bessie died from injuries sustained in a car accident. She was only 43, but she lived a full, hard life in her short years. This unparalleled singer experienced firsthand the highs and lows that were the subjects of her music. She triumphed over poverty and prejudice. She went from being a poor street singer to the celebrated "Empress of the Blues." Today, Bessie's many blues recordings are still considered some of the best of all time.

How Will You Rock the World?

"I have a passion for singing. I wouldn't have been able to audition for the choir if it hadn't been for Mrs. Wray, my music teacher, who saw my determination and how much I had practiced. With thanks to her, I will rock the world with my wonderful gift of singing."

Rachel Wullenweber, age 12

"I have always loved to sing — anywhere, anyplace, anytime. I am going to rock the world with the message of goodness to everyone in my songs."

Leeba Leider, age 14

Irène Joliot-Curie

1897–1956 ❧ CHEMIST ❧ FRANCE

I rène was surrounded by army doctors, medical equipment, and wounded soldiers. Blood was everywhere, and she could hear the battle raging in the distance over the cries of the sick and dying men around her. But eighteen-year-old Irène Curie was used to these horrifying distractions and focused her attention on setting up the new machine. The French doctors and nurses at the army hospital wondered what young Irène's mysterious contraption was all about.

When she finished setting up, Irène asked for a patient to volunteer. The doctors and nurses gasped in amazement as the soldier's leg bone magically appeared on the screen before them. They could see completely *inside* his leg — through the skin, the blood, and the muscle—right to the bone. And they could see exactly where the bone was broken. Irène was showing them the radioactive technology she and her mother had been working on—the groundbreaking X-ray machine!

Irène Curie was born to Nobel Prize-winning scientists Pierre and Marie Curie on September 12, 1897, in Paris. Her parents spent much of their time working, so she and her younger sister were largely raised by their grandfather, especially after Pierre's death in 1906. Irène was a quiet and thoughtful child who loved nature, poetry, and reading, but most of all, science. Although many girls were discouraged from studying math and science at the time, Marie Curie strongly supported her daughters' education in these subjects.

> *Irène was tall for her age and very athletic. Her favorite sports were biking, skiing, horseback riding, and mountain climbing, all of which she continued throughout her life.*
>
>

In fact, Marie considered most French schools too narrow in their academic offerings. So she started a cooperative school for her daughters and for eight other children of university professors. The professors themselves taught lessons in art, literature, science, math, English, and German. The cooperative school lasted only a couple of years, though, and after that Irène spent two years at a private girls' school. She later attended the prestigious Sorbonne University in Paris and received her doctoral degree for her studies of alpha particles in 1925.

Throughout her life, Irène was greatly inspired by her mother. Marie Curie was the first French woman to earn a doctoral degree, the first woman to teach at the Sorbonne, and the first woman in the world to win a Nobel Prize (she won two: the first in physics and the second in chemistry). Irène learned a lot from her mother, and they often worked together.

When World War I broke out in 1914, Irène and Marie put together X-ray units for the battlefront. Irène traveled to the French front lines to set them up and teach people how to use them. She showed doctors and nurses how to take X-rays of soldiers' wounds and locate bone breaks and pieces of shrapnel in the images. She then helped surgeons determine the best angle from which to enter the wounds for treatment.

After the war, Irène continued as her mother's assistant at the Radium Institute of the University of Paris. There she met her future husband and research partner, Fredéric Joliot. They married in 1926 and had two children: Hélène in 1927 and Pierre in 1932.

After their marriage, Irène and Frédéric began referring to themselves as the "Joliot-Curies." Together, they conducted groundbreaking experiments and wrote hundreds of reports. In 1934, Irène and Frédéric began experimenting with two metals, polonium and aluminum. Their results led them to a revolutionary discovery: they could create artificial radioactivity! This discovery earned Irène and Frédéric the 1935 Nobel Prize in chemistry. With this award, Irène and her mother, Marie, became the only mother and daughter to both win a Nobel Prize.

Sadly, Marie couldn't share in her daughter's triumph. At the time, no one knew how deadly it was to be exposed to radioactive chemicals. Because of her intense contact with these chemicals in her research, Marie died of leukemia one year before Irène's Nobel Prize was awarded.

After her mother's death, Irène took over the Radium Institute, and Frédéric started work as a scientist at the Collége de France. Irène joined several women's rights groups, speaking out in favor of a woman's right to hold a job *and* raise a family. In 1936, she became one of the first woman cabinet members in France when she was named as the under secretary of state for scientific research. She resigned from her office after only a few months, however, because politics took too much time away from her science.

Irène continued her research, and in 1938 she conducted another groundbreaking experiment. Although she considered her conclusions useless because they did not support what she was working on, later scientists repeated her experiment and realized that Irène had actually discovered nuclear fission (the splitting apart of atoms). Her results were analyzed by nuclear physicists and laid the crucial foundation for this important area of study.

Irène dedicated her life to her research and continued working in the laboratory until her death in 1956. Like her mother, she also died of leukemia, giving her life for her work. The French government organized a national funeral to honor the life of this great scientist who made some of the most significant scientific discoveries of her time.

Queen Salote Tupou III

1900–1965 ❋ *RULER OF TONGA* ❋ *TONGA*

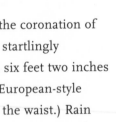

*Beyond her wisdom
and abilities there
was always her
strong affection for
her people, young
and old. Her love
for them was heart-
ily reciprocated.
Now, many years
after her death, the
Tongans still speak
of her as "Our
Beloved Queen."*
— Dr. A. H. Wood

Royal families from all over the world came to attend the coronation of Queen Elizabeth II, but Queen Salote Tupou III was startlingly different from the rest. This strong, passionate leader was six feet two inches tall and wore a traditional Tongan *ta'ovala* along with her European-style clothing. (A *ta'ovala* is a ceremonial matting worn around the waist.) Rain poured down on London the day of the coronation ceremony, but Queen Salote insisted on riding in an open carriage. She waved to the huge crowds lining the streets, and they cheered enthusiastically.

By the end of the journey, Queen Salote was soaked! When the astonished royalty asked why she had not allowed the carriage's hood to be raised, she smiled and charmingly explained that she thought it only fair to endure the rain just like the British citizens who had watched the procession through the downpour. She also told them that she was following an ancient Tongan tradition that one could not cover oneself when a higher-ranked ruler—in this case, the queen of England—was present. Queen Salote's preservation of tradition and her love for the people characterized her entire reign as ruler of Tonga.

Salote Mafile'o Pilolevu was born into the ruling family of Tonga, an island nation in the southwest Pacific Ocean, on March 13, 1900. When she was nine, she traveled to New Zealand to be educated. She returned to Tonga and got married when she was seventeen.

Salote's father died the next year, and she became queen of Tonga at the age of eighteen. She was officially crowned Salote Tupou III on October 11, 1918. At the coronation, she wore a *ta'ovala* that was handed down from her ancestors. The six-hundred-year-old *ta'ovala* was a symbol of the ancient gods.

At the time, Tonga was a British protectorate: an independent kingdom protected and influenced by England. During Queen Salote's rule, England's power over Tonga was decreased. However, Tonga's ties to England were still strong, and Queen Salote was often honored by the British government. In return, Tonga provided troops and support for England during World War II.

Queen Salote was greatly loved by her people because she worked hard to improve the country. She promoted agricultural development, health reform, and better living conditions and education for all Tongan people. She was especially interested in improving the welfare of women. The queen promoted education for girls, and she was active in the Pan-Pacific and South-East Asia Women's Association.

Queen Salote loved the ancient traditions of her country, and she advocated the preservation of Tongan culture. She formed and presided over an organization that encouraged the creation of traditional Tongan crafts for personal use and for sale to tourists. The queen formed the Tonga Traditions Committee in 1952.

Unlike most royalty, Queen Salote believed in having a strong connection with her people. She sent gifts to people in need, and her palace was open to everyone. Queen Salote celebrated Tongan culture through poetry and song. She wrote poems about history, tradition, nature, and everyday Tongan life. The poems were then set to music that she composed.

Dr. A. H. Wood, a friend of Queen Salote, wrote this about her:

> *In a procession three kilometres long 10,000 children were allowed to enter the Palace grounds and wave to the Queen as she sat on the verandah. Obviously in poor health, she nevertheless . . . received their greetings with undisguised delight. It was the last occasion on which the Tongan people saw their Queen.*[11]

December 16, 1965, was a sad day for the Tongan people. Early in the morning, their beloved Queen Salote died from cancer. A ruler for forty-seven years, Queen Salote enjoyed the longest reign in Tonga's history and will forever be remembered as a wise, gracious, and caring queen.

How Will You Rock the World?

"Being an American living in England, I have noticed that there are positives and negatives in every culture. People are more similar than not, and if we could accent the positives of all cultures, we would have a very strong world. I will rock the world as a teacher, helping my students open up to other cultures and ideas."

Emily Ricketson, age 11

Frida Kahlo

1907–1954 ❋ PAINTER ❋ MEXICO

*The only thing I
know is that I paint
because I need to.*
— Frida Kahlo

F rida rested in a bed at the Red Cross Hospital. The pain in her body was
agonizing—her spine was broken in three places, and her pelvis, right
leg, and foot were shattered! It was a miracle that the eighteen-year-old girl
was alive at all. The doctors hadn't expected her to survive after a streetcar
smashed into the bus she was riding. But she did survive, only to be wracked
with unbearable pain, night and day. As her body healed in the hospital,
Frida thought she would lose her mind. She could barely sleep, but being
awake was even worse — hours and hours with nothing but the pain!

After several months, in desperation, she had a nurse bring art supplies to her bed. As Frida concentrated on putting paint on the canvas, her mind no longer focused on the misery of her body. Her brush became an outlet for the physical and emotional pain she was enduring. Still in her teens, Frida had found her life's work, a career that would make her famous and respected throughout the world.

Frida Kahlo was born near Mexico City on July 6, 1907. She was one of five children of a German-Jewish photographer and a Mexican woman of Indian and Spanish descent. When she was fifteen, Frida was accepted into Mexico's prestigious National Preparatory School as one of thirty-five girls out of two thousand students. Frida was a bright girl; she studied literature and art, and she hoped to one day become a doctor.

> Frida had an endless curiosity about the world around her. She was known to cram all sorts of things into her school bag, including drawings, butterflies, dried flowers, and illustrated books from her father's library.

When she was eighteen years old, Frida's life was changed forever. She was in a horrible traffic accident, and overnight she went from a young, healthy, carefree girl to a girl who would struggle for the rest of her life with physical disabilities and pain. Fortunately, Frida found an outlet for her powerful emotions — painting.

Although she had no formal art training, Frida's work was strikingly mature. Her paintings, most of which were self-portraits, expressed her personal experiences and her complex feelings. In 1929, she married Diego Rivera, Mexico's most famous painter, whom she had met years before her accident while he was painting a mural at her school. Theirs was a passionate but stormy relationship. Frida's paintings captured her conflicting feelings for Diego and the pain of being childless. (She couldn't have children because of her injuries.) Frida's unique style drew upon popular Mexican art as well as surrealism. Using bright colors and powerful, symbolic images, Frida bared her soul to the world.

During the 1940s, Frida began showing her work internationally. Her raw, bold style was quite unusual and shocked most people who saw it. Despite this, her work won great critical acclaim. In 1953, she held her first major solo exhibition in Mexico City. It was a huge success. Although she was very ill at the time of her first exhibition, Frida insisted on being carried to the opening on a stretcher.

Several months later, Frida's health problems worsened, and one of her legs had to be amputated. But she found a way to make the best of the situation. Instead of being embarrassed and trying to hide her disability, she wore a red velvet boot with bells on her artificial leg.

Frida's health problems continued until her death in 1954. After she died, her home was made into the Frida Kahlo Museum. It holds not only Frida's original paintings but also her extensive collection of Mexican folk art. In 1985, the Mexican government declared Frida's paintings to be national treasures. The beautiful and vivid intensity of her art has earned her a place as one of the greatest artists in Mexico's history.

> *Because her ill health forced her to stay in bed for long periods of time, Frida surrounded herself with monkeys, dogs, parrots, and even frogs to keep her company!*
>
>

Andre Breton, a poet and art critic, indicates how the beauty of Frida's art often disguises its power; "The art of Frida Kahlo is a ribbon around a bomb."[12]

And Diego Rivera, Frida's husband, observes of her work; "Frida is the unique example in the history of art of someone who tore open the breast and heart in order to speak the biological truth of what is felt within them."[13]

How Will You Rock the World?

"I will rock the world by becoming a great and famous painter. I will paint inspiring pictures with joyful colors to decorate the walls of hospitals, schools, and nursing homes. My paintings will soothe and calm people, creating atmospheres that help learning, healing, and relaxing. The world will smile with my art."

Alta Brocha Mishvlovin, age 14

Mother Teresa

1910–1997 ✠ MISSIONARY TO THE POOR ✠ MACEDONIA AND INDIA

The poor do not need our compas-sion or our pity; they need our help. What they give to us is more than what we give to them.
— Mother Teresa

Young Agnes knelt in front of the cross. The church was empty and she was alone. She felt at peace as she gazed up at the statue of Jesus. She often thought about how he dedicated his life to serving the poor and loving the "unlovables"—the prostitutes, the handicapped, and all others who were outcast. For his work and his message of equality and forgiveness, he was killed. As she knelt before him, Agnes felt a strong conviction that stayed with her for the rest of her life. She too would help the poor and love the "unlovables." From that day forward, twelve-year-old Agnes knew that she would be a nun. This young girl's simple desire to help the unfortunate would eventually blossom into a global fight against poverty.

Agnes Gonxha Bojaxhiu was born on August 26, 1910, in Skopje, Macedonia. She was the youngest of three children born to an Albanian couple. Agnes's father died when she was still a young child, and her mother began making dresses to support the family. Agnes's mother also did charity work, and she took her daughter along on visits to the elderly, the sick, and the poor. A quiet and thoughtful child, Agnes enjoyed helping people in need. She was also deeply religious and often went alone to her Catholic church to pray.

Young Agnes had a beautiful voice and sang solos for the church choir.

By the age of twelve, Agnes had received her life's calling. She joined the Loreto nuns and traveled to Darjeeling, India, when she was only eighteen. After she took her first official vows as a nun and chose her new name, Sister Teresa (the patron saint of missionaries), she was sent to Calcutta to teach at St. Mary's, a school located in a convent and run by the nuns. Sister Teresa's work as a humanitarian had begun.

Sister Teresa worked at St. Mary's for twenty years, eventually becoming the principal. But she became increasingly disturbed by the horrible conditions of the people outside the convent walls. Calcutta's streets were crowded with homeless children, beggars, and lepers, many of them sick and starving. These were the people that Jesus loved and preached about.

On September 10, 1946, Sister Teresa was on a train going to Darjeeling when she received another call from God. This "call within a call," as she described it, told her that she was to leave the convent and the school and to help the poor while living among them. She could not disobey. She left the convent and went out into the streets of Calcutta.

Sister Teresa had a special love for children, so she immediately focused on helping the young people in the slums. She began by starting an informal school for them. In addition to basic language and math skills, Sister Teresa taught the children how to keep themselves clean in order to avoid certain diseases.

On the first day of her new "school," only five students joined Sister Teresa. She used a stick to scrape lessons in the dirt.

In 1950, Sister Teresa started her own order of nuns devoted to helping the poor. They were called the Missionaries of Charity. As the order's leader, she became "Mother" Teresa. The work was hard and the days were long, but young nuns poured in from around the world to join the new order. The nuns of the

Missionaries of Charity woke up at 4:30 A.M. to attend a worship service and eat breakfast. They went out into the city slums, where they worked until lunchtime. After lunch, they said their prayers and took a short rest. Then it was back to work until after dark.

The Missionaries of Charity continued to grow, largely due to the leadership and enthusiasm of Mother Teresa. In 1952, she opened Nirmal Hriday ("Pure Heart"), a home for the dying. Fatally ill patients were brought to the residence so they could die with peace and dignity. Mother Teresa then founded the first of her many orphanages, and she opened clinics for lepers and other people with severe disabilities. Over the years, Mother Teresa's work spread around the entire world.

During Mother Teresa's lifetime, the Missionaries of Charity opened facilities in five continents and ninety-five countries.

Mother Teresa's devotion to her cause brought her many awards and honors, which she accepted not for herself but on behalf of the poor and poverty-stricken throughout the world. Her awards included the Nobel Peace Prize, India's Padma Shri award, the U.S. Presidential Medal of Freedom, the Pope John XXIII Peace Prize, Great Britain's Templeton Prize for Progress in Religion, the Philippines' Magsaysay Award for International Understanding, and the Jewel of India Award.

The last few years of Mother Teresa's life were marked by lung, kidney, and heart problems, but she continued her missionary work. In 1997, she died at the age of eighty-seven, but the Missionaries of Charity are still working toward her humanitarian vision. Mother Teresa was respected and loved by rich and poor, young and old, in every corner of the globe. Millions of people mourned the passing of this visionary who had a special love for helping children: a modest woman who started her charitable work while still only a child herself.

Mary Leakey

1913–1996 ᴀʀᴄʜᴀᴇᴏʟᴏɢɪꜱᴛ ᴀɴᴅ ᴀɴᴛʜʀᴏᴘᴏʟᴏɢɪꜱᴛ

ᴇɴɢʟᴀɴᴅ ᴀɴᴅ ᴀꜰʀɪᴄᴀ

For me it was the sheer instinctive joy of collecting, or indeed one could say treasure hunting: it seemed that this whole area abounded in objects of beauty and great intrinsic interest that could be taken from the ground.

— Mary Leakey

Mary kneeled down over the ground, patiently and meticulously scanning the surface for fossils. Suddenly, something caught her attention. To most, it would look like just a dirty rock, but to Mary's trained eyes, it was a piece of human history. Bulging out from the ground was a fossilized bit of bone. Mary carefully brushed away the dirt around it to reveal two teeth and a curving jaw. Eventually, she would unearth more than four hundred pieces of the ancient skull. After the fragments were fitted together, analysis showed that the skull belonged to a pre-human ancestor who lived 1.75 million years ago. Mary's find proved that humanlike creatures existed much earlier than most scientists previously believed. This revolutionary discovery was just one of many important contributions Mary made to the study of archaeology.

Mary Nicol was born on February 6, 1913, in London, England. Her father was a landscape painter, but his true passion was archaeology. When Mary was still a young girl, he shared this love with her by taking her with him on expeditions to France. Young Mary learned how to excavate and use other techniques by assisting archaeologists as they uncovered and deciphered Stone Age cave paintings.

Mary didn't go to school like other children, but she learned how to read and draw from her father. Mary was only thirteen years old when he died. At first her mother tried sending her to convent schools, but Mary wasn't used to learning in a traditional school environment. After Mary was expelled from two institutions, her mother gave up.

Meanwhile, Mary was learning in her own way by attending lectures at museums and universities. When she was just seventeen, Mary assisted at an archaeological site in southern England. It was there that she met archaeologist Dorothy Liddell. Dorothy showed Mary that women could be successful in archaeology, a traditionally male-dominated field. Encouraged, Mary began sketching high-quality pictures of the tools at the site.

One day another archaeologist, Gertrude Caton-Thompson, saw young Mary's drawings. She was very impressed and asked Mary to draw some ancient tools that had been discovered in Egypt. Gertrude introduced Mary to Louis Leakey, an anthropologist who worked in Africa. Louis was writing a book on his work and asked Mary to illustrate it. Mary joined him in Africa and began working on the illustrations and on the dig site. Working side by side and sharing their mutual passion for archaeology, it wasn't long before Mary and Louis fell in love. In 1936, they got married.

Over the next few years, Mary and Louis worked in various sites in Africa. Among Mary's finds were a cremation ground, ancient tools, and pottery. She made her first famous discovery in 1948, when she dug up the eighteen-million-year-old skull of a pre-human ancestor.

In 1959, Mary made perhaps the greatest find of her career: the skull of a human predecessor that was 1.75 million years old. Before Mary's discovery, scientists believed that humanlike creatures had existed for only several hundred thousand years. Mary's discovery proved them all wrong!

Soon after that, she discovered a set of ancient humanlike footprints that were 3.7 million years old. This proved that early human ancestors walked upright much earlier than scientists previously thought.

Mary continued to live in Africa until her death in 1996. Her ground-breaking work opened the door for girls of the future who wanted to grow up to be archaeologists, scientists, and adventurers. Through Mary's archaeological explorations and expertise, theories about the history of human development were changed forever. She remarked:

> *What I have done in my life I have done because I wanted to do it and because it interested me. I just happen to be a woman, and I don't believe it has made much of a difference.*[14]

How Will You Rock the World?

"I will rock the world by becoming a famous photographer. I will travel to remote locations like Africa, Asia, and maybe even into space, taking pictures of all my journeys."

Aaliyah Muhammad, age 12

"When I grow up I want to be a pig farmer and an astronaut. I will rock the world by being the first person to take pigs into space."

Ellen Yecny, age 7

Babe Didrikson

*She is the most
flawless section
of muscle harmony,
of complete mental
and physical
coordination the
world of sports
has ever known.*
— Grantland Rice,
sportswriter

I t was Babe's first basketball game playing for the Golden Cyclones, a semiprofessional team. They were playing the national champions, the Sun Oil team, and her teammates were nervous. But Babe wasn't nervous. She ran and passed and shot the ball, again and again and again. By the end, the Golden Cyclones had won the game. Babe had scored more baskets than the entire Sun Oil team combined! The other girls were amazed by the eighteen-year-old super-athlete, but they had no idea that Babe would become one of the greatest athletes of all time. She excelled at almost every sport she tried, including golf, track, baseball, archery, skeet shooting, swimming, diving, horseback riding, and billiards, to name just a few. Her life set an inspiring example for all female athletes who followed in her footsteps.

Mildred Ella Didrikson was born on June 26, 1914, in Port Arthur, Texas.

Her family was very poor, and she and her six brothers and sisters all had to help out. Mildred picked figs and sewed pototo sacks for money. Sports were her way of having fun. Early on she decided that she would be the greatest athlete ever.

As a young girl, she was such a powerful home-run hitter that kids nicknamed her "Babe" after the famous slugger Babe Ruth. Her father built a gym in the backyard, and out of all her brothers and sisters, Babe used it the most. She worked out on the gym's chin-up bars and weight-lifting equipment. She also played baseball and basketball with the kids in the neighborhood.

In high school, Babe went out for every sport open to girls. She earned a spot on the basketball team and soon became a star. Her athletic ability

There were several rows of hedges in Babe's neighborhood, which she loved jumping over during her runs. Later she would earn an Olympic gold medal in the hurdles.

attracted the attention of Melvin Coombs, the manager of a company-sponsored women's basketball team. He recruited Babe to play on his team, the Golden Cyclones, and she led them to a national championship. In 1930, she was voted all-American forward.

Babe decided to try track and field next. In 1932, she competed in the Amateur Athletic Union women's national championship. Out of eight events, Babe won five, tied for first in another, and took second in another. Babe earned enough points to win the *team* title all by herself!

Her outstanding track victories at the national championship led Babe to the 1932 Olympics in Los Angeles. As she left for the games, she told reporters that she planned "to beat everybody in sight." And beat them she did. Babe won a gold medal and set the world record in the javelin throw, won another gold medal in the hurdles, and won a silver medal in the high jump!

While she was in Los Angeles, Babe played her first round of golf. Her natural ability was impressive. A few years later, Babe decided to make a career out of the sport. She practiced hard, sometimes for fifteen or sixteen hours a day, and her hard work paid off when she won the

When Babe returned to Texas after the Olympics, she rode into her hometown in the fire chief's car at the head of a parade held in her honor. They gave her the key to the city.

75

Texas Women's Amateur Golf Tournament in 1935. She remembered:

> *Weekends I put in twelve and sixteen hours a day on golf . . . .*
> *I'd drill and drill and drill on the different kinds of shots. I'd*
> *hit balls until my hands were bloody and sore . . . . After it got*
> *too late to practice any more, I went home and had my dinner.*
> *Then I'd go to bed with the golf rule book.*[15]

In 1937, Babe met wrestler George Zaharias at a golf tournament, and the two were married in less than a year. Babe continued her golf career, winning an incredible seventeen tournaments in a row! She was the first American to win the British Women's Amateur Tournament. But Babe's biggest impact on women's golf was yet to come. In 1949, she helped to found the Ladies' Professional Golf Association. This organization sponsored professional women's golf tournaments, which attracted more and more women to the sport. Today, LPGA tournaments offer millions of dollars in prize money for professional woman golfers.

Babe wrote this in her autobiography:

> *Before I was even into my teens, I knew exactly what I wanted*
> *to be when I grew up. My goal was to be the greatest athlete*
> *that ever lived. I suppose I was born with the urge to get into*
> *sports, and the ability to do pretty well at it.*
>
> *Now there's nobody who wants to win more than I do. I'll*
> *knock myself out to do it. But I've never played rough or dirty.*
> *To me good sportsmanship is just as important as winning . . . .*
> *You have to play the game the right way. If you win through*
> *bad sportsmanship, that's no real victory in my book.*[16]

In 1953, Babe was diagnosed with cancer. She fought the disease with her usual determination, and after undergoing surgery, Babe recovered and miraculously won the U.S. Open Golf Tournament in 1954. Babe persevered like a champion for two more years, but in 1956 the cancer returned. The world's greatest female athlete died at the age of 42.

Throughout her life, Babe earned prestigious awards and honors. She was the only woman to be named the Associated Press's "Woman Athlete of the Year" six times! She was also voted the "Woman Athlete of the Half Century" in 1950. Sports historians ranked her as the second most outstanding and influential athlete in American sports history, just after Babe Ruth. Babe Didrikson's legacy has passed on to today's female athletes. Her talent and determination opened doors for women to compete and succeed in the world of sports.

How Will You Rock the World?

"When two professional baseball players came to my school, we asked them if there were ever girls on the team. Their answer was 'No.' I will rock the world by being

the first girl baseball, hockey, or basketball player on a team with boys. Girls who want to play sports should be considered girls who rock the world."

Miranda Begley, age 9

"I have been skiing since I was four years old. I am going to rock the world by being a ski

instructor or even a professional skier. Later I will own my own ski hill."

Andrée Dion, age 10

Indira Gandhi

1917–1984 🔲 *RULER OF INDIA* 🔲 *INDIA*

*I cannot under-
stand how anyone
can be an Indian
and not be proud —
the richness and
infinite variety of
our composite
heritage, the
magnificence of the
people's spirit,
equal to any
disaster or burden,
firm in their faith,
gay spontaneously
even in poverty
and hardship.*

— Indira Gandhi

Twelve-year-old Indira sat nervously with her schoolbooks in the back-seat of a car. She had just left a secret meeting where the top leaders of India's National Congress Party were planning the next step in their rebellion against the British. At that time, India was a British colony, and India's people were struggling to gain their independence.

As Indira's car reached the tall iron gates, a police inspector ordered her driver to stop. Indira's heart raced. If the police searched the car she would be caught and put in jail along with many leaders of the rebellion. The brave girl hid her fear by impatiently demanding that the inspector let her pass; she was late for school and had no time for these delays. The police believed her and let her go. Little did they know that hidden safely in her trunk were all the secret documents of the independence movement!

As her car passed through the gate, Indira looked out the back window and saw that the police had already surrounded the house. Inside, the leaders watched nervously as Indira's car escaped. Fearing a raid on their headquarters, the Indian leaders had placed all their most important papers in the trunk of the young girl's car. It was vital that the British not get their hands on those documents, and thanks to Indira, they were safe. This daring act of bravery was just the beginning of Indira's career of devotion to her country: the twelve-year-old girl would go on to become the first woman leader of a democracy and one of the most powerful and influential politicians in the world.

Indira Priyadarshini Nehru was born on November 19, 1917, in Allahabad, India. Her country had been ruled by England for over 160 years. The British invaders controlled everything and Indian citizens had little to no power in their own country. Any Indians who spoke out in favor of Indian independence were thrown in jail. As the only child of Jawaharlal and Kamala Nehru, leaders in India's struggle for independence, Indira spent a lot of her childhood without her parents. Her mother and father were often in jail. But their work inspired Indira, who, even as a child, loved India with a passion and did all she could to help the revolutionary National Congress Party.

When Indira was twelve, she organized more than one thousand Indian children into a group

> Indira's earliest memory was of her family burning clothes and other items made outside India in a nonviolent boycott of European goods. Little Indira threw her own European-made doll into the flames.

called the Monkey Brigade. They helped the Congress Party in everyday tasks like addressing envelopes, writing announcements, and cooking food. More importantly, Indira's group spied on the British police. While they pretended to play, the children would eavesdrop on police conversations, listening for news of any upcoming arrests. Then they reported back to the Congress Party. By giving activists time to hide, the Monkey Brigade's early warnings often prevented arrests. The police never suspected that this group of innocent-looking kids were actually spies!

In 1937, Indira was accepted into Oxford University in England. While studying in England, Indira got engaged to a childhood friend, Feroze Gandhi, and the two were married when they returned to India in 1942.

Upon her arrival back in India, Indira found her beloved country in the midst of the bloodiest fighting of the entire rebellion. She immediately dove back into her work in the party, and it wasn't long before the British learned of her rebellious activities. Young Indira was thrown in prison for nine months! But she didn't lose hope. She and the other activists were making great progress. In 1947, the British gave up the fight. After almost two hundred years of colonialism, India finally won its independence!

England was fighting World War II while Indira studied there. She drove an ambulance to help with the British war effort. But back in India, the British had put her father in jail again at the exact same time.

As the most popular leader in the National Congress Party, Indira's father became the first prime minister of India after the war. Indira's mother died in 1936, so Indira acted as her father's "first lady," advisor, and ambassador to other countries. She was still active in many political organizations, and in 1959 she was elected president of the National Congress Party. This was a post both her father and grandfather had held; it made her the second-highest-ranking politician in India.

When Indira's father died in 1964, Lal Shastri became prime minister, and he appointed Indira as minister of information and broadcasting. In a country where few people could read, radio and television held great power for bringing news and information to *all* the people of India, not just the rich and educated. Indira made great progress by doubling the number of radio and television pro-

Indira's hero was Joan of Arc, who also fought for her country's independence from invaders.

grams, producing inexpensive radios, and creating a family-planning program. She was also the first person to open up the airwaves to *anyone* who wished to speak; even critics of the government were free to voice their ideas. India was becoming a true democracy.

Two years later, Shastri died, and Indira was elected prime minister of India. She was the first woman ever to run a democratic country—and the world's most populated and diverse democracy at that! Her newly independent country was plagued with problems and threats to its freedom. Many people didn't think she could handle the responsibility, and even some members of the National Congress Party initially thought she would be easy for them to manipulate. But Indira proved to be a powerful and skillful leader.

During her term, Indira strengthened India's international influence and kept both the United States and the Soviet Union from exerting their control over her nation. She led India to victory in a bloody war with Pakistan and sent the country's first satellite into space. At home she launched a "Remove Poverty" campaign to help limit population growth and improve the quality of life for India's poorer citizens. Indira was re-elected in 1971, despite some growing opposition.

Throughout Indira's second term as prime minister, criticism of her policies mounted steadily. She had created *voluntary* sterilization to help limit the population and curb poverty, but her enemies claimed it was *forced*. In 1975, riots and protests against her became so severe that Indira declared a state of emergency. She imprisoned political opponents and censored the press. Though these short-term undemocratic practices were no longer in effect by the 1977 election, Indira was voted out of office. She spent the next two years regaining support and was re-elected by a landslide in 1979.

Indira continued her work to improve the country she loved, but she still faced strong opposition. In 1984, she ordered a raid on a temple held by extremists from the Sikh religion. The Sikh community retaliated with violent force, and Indira was assassinated by her two Sikh bodyguards.

Indira's will was found after her assassination. She said:

> *If I die a violent death as some fear and a few are plotting,*
> *I know the violence will be in the thought and action of the*
> *assassin, not in my dying—for no hate is dark enough to over-*
> *shadow the extent of my love for my people and my country.*[17]

Though her time as a leader was full of controversy, Indira helped her nation through the transition from colonial rule to democracy. She ruled during a challenging and trouble-plagued time in India's history. Through it all, her love of her country and its people was clear, and her intentions to promote the welfare of India prevailed. A strong and confident woman, Indira left her mark as a powerful leader who aspired to advance one of the largest, poorest, and most diverse democracies in the world.

Anne Frank

1929–1945 🌿 *DIARIST* 🌿 *GERMANY AND THE NETHERLANDS*

*Her voice was
preserved out of the
millions that were
silenced . . . . It
has outlasted the
shouts of the mur-
derers and has
soared above the
voices of time.*
— Ernst Schnabel

Anne looked around the dimly lit room. She and her family had been
hiding from the Nazis for over two years, and they had to be extremely
careful. Their hiding place was in a room over a warehouse. During the day
they had to be completely silent, barely moving in their rooms and speaking
only in tiny whispers, if at all. Any noise could mean discovery by the
workers below. But Anne felt lucky that she had her family and a few friends
hiding with her. Many Jews were not so lucky.

Anne tried to make her attic hiding place as nice as possible; she hung
postcards and pictures of movie stars on the wall. But it wasn't really like
home at all. The closest Anne could get to the outside world was to listen
softly to the radio at night. But Anne had another way of escaping — her
diary. In it, she wrote her thoughts, feelings, experiences, and her dreams,

leaving a treasured record of her life as a Jewish girl during the Holocaust.

Annelies Marie Frank was born on June 12, 1929, in Frankfurt, Germany. When Anne was just four years old, the Nazi Party gained control of her country. Their racist teachings called for the brutal oppression of Jews, and eventually, the Nazis sought to wipe the entire Jewish race off the face of the earth. In 1934, Anne and her family tried to escape Nazi persecution by moving to Amsterdam in the Netherlands.

Anne's father, Otto, started a new business, and things went well for a few years. But in 1940, the Germans took control of Amsterdam, and life for the Franks changed radically. In 1942, Anne's older sister was ordered to report to the Nazis so they could send her away to a concentration camp. The Franks knew families that had been sent to concentration camps, and none of them had ever been heard from again. The Frank family decided to go into hiding in a few rooms above Otto's business warehouse. They also hid another family and a friend. This was a risky choice, but they knew it was the only way the family could stay together. Anne was only thirteen years old.

When the Franks first escaped to their hiding place, they had to wear several outfits of clothing at once. Jews couldn't walk safely through the city streets with suitcases. Anne thought she would suffocate during that terrifying trip.

For the next two years, Anne and the others never dared to leave their hideout. They received food and other supplies from Dutch friends who risked their own lives by helping Jews. Anne often wrote in her beloved diary. She had been given the red-and-white-checkered journal for her thirteenth birthday, and it was one of the few things she was able to take with her into hiding. On September 28, 1942, Anne wrote:

> So far you truly have been a great source of comfort to me and now I can hardly wait for those moments when I'm able to write in you. Oh I'm so glad I brought you along.[18]

In August 1944, just after Anne's fifteenth birthday, a warehouse worker told the German police about the Franks' hiding place. Their hideout was raided and everyone was arrested and sent to concentration camps. Of the eight people who hid above the warehouse, only Anne's father survived the horrifying ordeal. Anne died of typhoid in the Bergen-Belson concentration camp shortly before her sixteenth birthday.

When Anne's father returned to Amsterdam after the war, their brave Dutch friends gave him his daughter's diary. The Nazis had trashed the hideout during the raid, but the friends had managed to save Anne's book of memories. Otto Frank published his daughter's diary in 1947.

Today Anne's diary survives as the voice of an ordinary girl facing a horrible tragedy. Her words are proof of our capacity for courage and hope, even in the worst of times. On May 3, 1944, Anne wrote:

Anne always dreamed of becoming a writer. She wrote short stories, fables, and essays. Anne's diary was translated into over thirty languages and made into a Pulitzer Prize-winning play.

> *I've made up my mind to lead a different life from other girls.*
> *What I'm experiencing here is a good beginning to an interest-*
> *ing life and that's the reason, the only reason, why I have to*
> *laugh at the humorous side of the most dangerous moments.*[19]

The Nazis never crushed the spirit of this extraordinary girl. In one of her last diary entries, Anne writes, "In spite of everything, I still believe that people are really good at heart."

How Will You Rock the World?

"Photography is a great way to express yourself. I will rock the world by taking pictures of people during hard times. My photographs and lectures will teach people all around the world how to help one another."

Erica Zora Wrightson, age 12

Wilma Rudolph

1940–1994 ✳ OLYMPIC ATHLETE ✳ UNITED STATES

I loved the feeling of freedom in running, the fresh air, the feeling that the only person I'm competing with is me.

— Wilma Rudolph

Ten-year-old Wilma hung back as the congregation filed into the church building. Almost everyone she knew in Clarksville was there. As her friends and family sat down in the pews, Wilma unbuckled the leg brace that she'd worn for six years. Laying it aside, she took a deep breath and stepped through the church doors. Whispers rose as Wilma, who hadn't been seen without her brace since she was four years old, bravely walked down the aisle. As she took her seat, Wilma's pride mingled with the joy of the congregation. She had actually walked the full length of the church. Though her life would be filled with victories, today was one of Wilma's biggest triumphs. Little did the congregation dream that in days to come, this courageous girl would become known as the "fastest woman in the world"!

Wilma Rudolph was born on June 23, 1940, in Bethlehem, Tennessee.

She was the twentieth of twenty-two children born to Ed and Blanche Rudolph. In her early childhood, Wilma battled measles, mumps, chicken pox, pneumonia, and scarlet fever. When she was four, she contracted polio, a crippling disease that left her unable to control the muscles in her left leg.

Wilma was told that she would never walk again, but she and her family refused to believe the diagnosis. Over the next ten years, they worked together to prove the doctors wrong. Wilma's brothers and sisters took turns massaging and exercising her leg every day. Twice a week, Wilma and her mother rode the bus to a hospital for physical-therapy treatments that would strengthen her muscles. At that time, the southern United States was racially segregated, and the nearest hospital that accepted African-Americans was fifty miles away in Nashville.

Of her diagnosis, Wilma said, "The doctor told me I would never walk, but my mother told me I would, so I believed my mother."

Wilma and her mother were forced to ride in the back of the bus all the way.

With such a supportive family, Wilma made slow but encouraging progress. When she was seven, her leg was strong enough that she could walk with the help of a special brace. This meant that she could finally go to school with her brothers and sisters. Wilma still couldn't participate in games and sports like the other kids, however, so she was determined to get even stronger.

By the time Wilma was ten, she could walk short distances without the aid of her brace. Two years later, she joyfully mailed the brace back to the hospital in Nashville. She even began to play basketball! In the seventh grade, Wilma earned a spot on the school team, and over the next few years, she became a star player. During her sophomore year of high school, she scored a phenomenal 803 points in twenty-five games! This was a new record for Tennessee girls' basketball.

Wilma's amazing talent caught the attention of Ed Temple, a women's track coach from Tennessee State University. Temple was impressed with her speed and determination, and he invited her to attend a summer track program at Tennessee State. This gave her a wonderful opportunity to practice and improve her skills. And practice she did. In 1956, she was such a fast runner that she qualified for the United States Olympic track team! The Olympics were held in Melbourne, Australia, and young Wilma had barely traveled outside of Clarksville, Tennessee. She was thrilled! Only sixteen years old and the youngest member of the team, Wilma nevertheless won a bronze medal in the 400-meter relay.

Wilma resolved to compete in the next Olympics, and four years later, at the 1960 Olympic Games in Rome, she made history. With her stunning victories in the 100-meter dash, the 200-meter dash, and the 400-meter relay, Wilma became the first American woman runner to win three gold medals. She was officially dubbed the "fastest woman in the world."

Wilma received many other prestigious awards for her incredible athletic skill. She was voted Woman Athlete of the Year by the Associated Press and was named Sportsman of the Year by a group of European sportswriters. By the time she retired from track in 1962, she had won the James E. Sullivan Award for good sportsmanship and the Babe Didrikson Zaharias Award, an honor bestowed on the best female athletes in the world.

When Wilma returned to her hometown after her Olympic victories, she was greeted by cheers and banners. The town even held a parade in her honor. The parade, attended by both African-American and white citizens, was the first integrated event in Clarksville's history!

In 1963, Wilma graduated from Tennessee State University with a degree in elementary education. She became a schoolteacher, track coach, and director of children's sports programs. In 1967, she joined Operation Champ, an organization of athletes who coached children and teens from the inner cities. In the late 1970s, Wilma founded her own company, Wilma Unlimited, and traveled around the country giving inspirational speeches. She shared her own story of triumph and encouraged kids to pursue their dreams no matter what obstacles they faced. Wilma was passionate about encouraging young athletes, and in 1981 she founded the Wilma Rudolph Foundation to train young people in sports.

Tom Biracree wrote:

> *Wilma Rudolph had overcome polio and risen from poverty to become the "fastest woman in the world." She had won respect for women in the male-dominated world of sports, through her own spectacular achievements. Yet, Rudolph told [a] journalist*

that she valued her own idealism as much as any of her unique accomplishments: "I just want to be remembered as a hard-working lady with certain beliefs."[20]

In 1994, Wilma Rudolph died of a brain tumor. A gifted athlete and a determined competitor, she inspired many with her remarkable courage and talent. Her life is an inspiration to everyone who has a dream that seems impossible. Wilma's hard work and triumph prove that with determination and vision, even the most devastating setbacks can be overcome.

How Will You Rock the World?

"With my passion for designing clothing, I will rock this world as kids from all across the country dance and play in jeans by TISHA. Then

I will take my first million and house the homeless. Then, and only then, will I feel I have rocked the world!"

Tisha Nicole Khakazi, age 14

"I'm going to rock the world by making Xeno Transplantation possible. The transplantation of animal organs into the bodies of humans

will allow the thousands of people who wouldn't have gotten human transplants to live long, healthy lives."

Dena Gordon, age 15

Susan Eloise (S. E.) Hinton

1950— ✳ NOVELIST ✳ UNITED STATES

When I was young,
girls never got to
do anything. They
got to rat their
hair and outline
their eyes in black,
but that was
about the extent of
their activities.
— S. E. Hinton

S usan Hinton watched as actor Matt Dillon performed a scene taken from her novel *Tex*. She still couldn't believe that her book was going to become a movie. Her teenage fans had demanded it—they wrote so many letters to producers, begging that they make the movie, that Hollywood finally listened. Other movies followed, like *Rumble Fish*; *That Was Then, This Is Now*; and one based on Susan's most famous novel, *The Outsiders*, which was directed by Francis Ford Coppola and starred Matt Dillon, Emilio Estevez, Ralph Macchio, Patrick Swayze, and Tom Cruise.

Susan was very involved in the process of turning her books into movies. She wanted everything to be right, so she helped with casting, screenwriting, and directing. As a fifteen-year-old girl writing her first novel, *The Outsiders*, Susan never imagined that she would be published in just two years, that her stories would become some of the most popular books for teens ever, or that she would help turn them into movies.

The film The Outsiders is dedicated to the students and librarians who requested that the book be made into a movie.

Susan Eloise Hinton was born in Tulsa, Oklahoma, in 1950. As a child, she loved to read, and she dreamed about becoming a writer. Her first writings were about cowboys and horses. Susan's father died when she was in high school. She was close to him, and as he got sicker and sicker, she turned more and more to her writing.

While attending Will Rogers High School, Susan wrote *The Outsiders*. She began her first draft when she was just fifteen, and by the time the novel was published two years later, she had rewritten the book four times! At the age of seventeen, Susan became an overnight success. Unlike most other books at the time, her novel dealt with the reality of life for many teenagers. Although some people criticized the book for being too violent, most praised it for its true-to-life depiction of teen conflict.

The Outsiders tells the story of Ponyboy Curtis and his "greaser" friends as they fight against the "socs" (short for "socials") and struggle to find their place in the world. Susan got her inspiration for the book from witnessing the real conflict between "greasers" and "socs" in her own hometown. She was bothered by the way many of her peers judged each other solely by appearance and income.

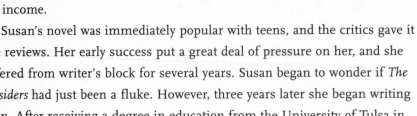

The same year The Outsiders was published, Susan received a D in her creative-writing class!

Susan's novel was immediately popular with teens, and the critics gave it rave reviews. Her early success put a great deal of pressure on her, and she suffered from writer's block for several years. Susan began to wonder if *The Outsiders* had just been a fluke. However, three years later she began writing again. After receiving a degree in education from the University of Tulsa in 1971, Susan published her second novel. *That Was Then, This Is Now* is also about teen conflict, violence, and troubled homes. Susan continued to work with this theme, publishing *Rumble Fish* in 1975, *Tex* in 1979, and *Taming the Star Runner* in 1988. All of her novels were well-received, and four were made into successful movies.

Susan's first four novels were written in the first person, with a boy narrating the story. She said she "became" the narrator as she told the story and felt more comfortable writing from a boy's perspective. This may be because boys were some of her closest friends while growing up. She used her initials, "S. E.," while writing her books because when she published *The Outsiders*, she didn't want readers to know she was a girl. She was afraid that no one would believe that a girl could really know anything about gangs, abusive parents, or peer pressure from a boy's point of view.

Susan's novels are still read and enjoyed by millions of teenagers each year. Recently, she started writing children's books. Her picture book, *Big David, Little David*, came out in 1994, and *The Puppy Sister* was published in 1995. Susan's books have won countless awards, such as the American Library Association's Best Books for Young Adults and the *School Library Journal*'s Best Books of the Year. Susan was also the first recipient of the Margaret Edwards Author Achievement Award for her success in reaching her young-adult audience. Susan was one of the first authors to write realistically about the conflicts and concerns of teens. Her style has influenced the genre of young-adult literature forever.

How Will You Rock the World?

"I will rock the world by writing screenplays. I would like to make people laugh when I write something funny and cry when I write something sad. Even if I just make one person feel better by watching my movies, I'll know I did well."

Maureen Gualtieri, age 12

Amatalrauf al-Sharki ("Raufa Hassan")

1958– ◻ CELEBRITY AND WOMEN'S RIGHTS ACTIVIST ◻ YEMEN

Inside me I didn't like that veil anymore. I felt it was a big lie. I wanted to be me. Just me, accepted the way I was . . . . I began to realise that the veil was just something to hold me back in life and not really for my benefit. Since then this started to rage inside me . . . . I had become a different person.
— Raufa Hassan

I t was 1975, and television had just come to the country of Yemen. Seventeen-year-old Amatalrauf al-Sharki, famous with the Yemeni public as radio personality "Raufa Hassan," was about to appear in one of the first Yemeni television programs. After all, Raufa had been the star of her own successful radio show since she was twelve. But this was entirely different — for the first time her country would *see* her. And she had quite a surprise for them.

Raufa had just returned from her first year of college and had vowed to stop wearing her traditional veil. It was the custom of most Islamic women,

92

especially in Yemen, to wear the veil in public at all times to conceal themselves from the view of men. While Raufa went to college in the less-traditional country of Egypt, she came to believe that the veil was a symbol which held women back from achieving equality. To her, it was a form of discrimination. If she wore it, Raufa would feel she was lying to herself and her country. She wouldn't do it.

When the cameras began rolling, all of Yemen saw the face of their favorite female celebrity. Many viewers were shocked, including Raufa's family and friends, but Raufa stood by her beliefs. By not wearing a veil, Raufa publicly asserted her independence and began a personal campaign to promote women's rights in Islamic countries.

Amatalrauf al-Sharki was born in 1958 in a North Yemeni town called Ibb. By the time she was in the sixth grade, she had begun her work in the media. Her first job was singing in a children's radio show, but she quickly moved on to bigger things. One day, a broadcaster didn't show up for his program at the radio station, and Amatalrauf agreed to fill in for him. The twelve-year-old girl did such a good job as his replacement that she was asked to be an official broadcaster with her own show!

However, Amatalrauf was sure that her father would be angry if she had her own radio show. He would consider it a scandal if his daughter were publicly speaking over the airwaves. But Amatalrauf was determined to have her own show, so she and the other station employees worked out a way for her to continue on the radio. She simply changed her broadcasting name so that no one would know who she was. Amatalrauf did tell her mother, who saw no real harm in the idea and was happy that her daughter would be earning an income. From that day on, Amatalrauf became known to the Yemeni public as Raufa Hassan.

Each day, Raufa would go to the radio station after school to record her broadcasts. Her plan worked well until six months later, when an announcer accidentally introduced her as "Raufa Hassan *al-Sharki*." Her secret identity was ruined! Raufa's father threatened to not let her work anymore, but he eventually backed down and allowed Raufa to continue her show.

Raufa's broadcasts were different from most. For three years, she had a program about family topics. While other such programs dealt with women's household duties as a wife, Raufa emphasized that family responsibilities belong to both men *and* women. Even as a teen, she promoted equality between the sexes.

Over the next few years, Raufa became more involved in the women's movement, participating in activities and organizations that advocated women's rights. She was active in the Yemeni Women's Association until a religious group shut it down in 1973. That same year, at age fifteen, she and three friends founded a school to teach Yemeni girls and women to read and write. This was a major step for education in Yemen, where over 70 percent of the women were illiterate. Raufa also shocked the public when she marched in a Yemeni military parade. She and a group of girls trained for three weeks, learning how to walk in formation and carry guns. They were the first women to participate in the Day of the Revolution celebration, previously an all-male activity.

But perhaps Raufa's most significant actions centered around the question of whether or not to wear a veil. Like most other Yemeni women, she was brought up with the tradition of covering her face except for her eyes. During her radio broadcasts, though, she couldn't wear a veil because it would muffle her voice. Raufa decided to keep this a secret; she knew it would be offensive to many people — especially her family — if they knew she performed her broadcasts without a veil. Only the people at the station knew about it, and she didn't even let many of them see her face uncovered. During her five years at the station, only the program producer and the station engineer were allowed to watch while she recorded her broadcasts. Inside, though, Raufa was becoming more and more uncomfortable with wearing her veil. She began to see it as a device that held her back as a woman.

In 1975, Raufa graduated from high school. Despite opposition from her family, she attended the University of Cairo in Egypt, where she studied information and mass communication. When Raufa returned from her freshman year, she no longer wore a veil. This came as a shock to her family and friends, who were even more amazed when she appeared on television without her veil. Soon Raufa became well-known throughout the country for her controversial "unveiled" television broadcasts.

Raufa continued her education and her work as a women's rights advocate. In 1977, she restarted the Yemeni Women's Association and became its president two years later. She eventually earned a master's degree in mass communication from the University of Norwich and a doctorate from the University of Paris.

Since that time, Raufa has worked as a professor and a leader in the campaign for women's rights. In 1993, Raufa ran for Parliament in Yemen's first democratic elections. Though she lost, she continues to make a difference in Yemeni politics, inspiring women to be more politically active. She helped form the Arab Democratic Institute, an organization that promotes women's voting projects. The group encourages Yemeni women, especially those in rural areas, to use their votes and let their voices be heard. In the 1997 Yemeni elections, the ADI financed campaigns for nine women candidates for Parliament.

Raufa is making progress in her attempts to give Yemeni women more power, but she has a tough road ahead of her. Traditionally, women's roles have been restrictive and submissive. Even today, girls in Yemen are encouraged to marry in their teens, setting motherhood as their only lifetime goal and hoping for many children. Education, careers, and anything that takes girls or women into the public is discouraged or even forbidden. Illiteracy among Yemeni women is still disturbingly high.

Raufa's work is far from done, but she continues her fight. From an early age, she showed independence and leadership in promoting women's rights, a cause to which she has devoted much of her life. Today, Raufa's achievements have made her one of the most important and influential feminists in the Arab world. She challenges the ways in which her choices are restricted and expands what is possible for women in her country.

How Will You Rock the World?

"Every day the news on television is filled with stories that make me think that people need to get along better. I will rock the world by being a police officer and a role model. We need more police officers who are women and who are from different races, religions, and cultures."

Elana Goldstein, age 8

Nadia Comaneci

1961– ✳ OLYMPIC GYMNAST ✳ ROMANIA AND THE UNITED STATES

Nadia showed her boldness, courage, and abilities, even in the workouts. She went through the most unbeliev-able stunts. She did neckbreaking somersaults on the uneven high bar. She swung so high and far out that viewers thought she would miss the bars.
— Gloria Miklowitz

A huge crowd watched as Nadia began her routine on the uneven bars. At just four feet eleven inches tall, the young girl didn't appear especially strong or powerful. But fourteen-year-old Nadia had been training in gymnastics for years and building up the strength and stamina that she needed to be successful in her sport. Through hours of practice and hundreds of ballet lessons, she had also learned to be smooth and graceful in her movements. Now she was ready to put it all together for her performance in the 1976 Olympic Games.

Her turn arrived, and she stood for a moment near the bars, concentrating on the routine ahead of her. In a flash, Nadia grasped the low bar and swung up to the high bar, where she began a stunning series of handstands, revolutions, and release moves. The audience was breathless for a moment after her twisting dismount, but they soon responded with a standing ovation. A few seconds later, the judges announced Nadia's score. She had earned a perfect 10—the first ever awarded in Olympic competition! For the rest of the Olympics, Nadia continued to wow audiences and judges alike, receiving six more perfect 10s before the competition was over.

Nadia Comaneci was born on November 12, 1961, in Onesti, Romania. She began her career as a gymnast when coach Bela Karolyi visited her kindergarten classroom. He was looking for talented girls to participate in his gymnastics program. When Bela asked Nadia and her classmates if any of them liked gymnastics, Nadia enthusiastically yelled out that she did. After she passed a test of her abilities, including running, jumping, and walking across a balance beam, Nadia began her training with Bela.

At that time in Romania, most young athletes trained at special schools, where they lived away from their families. At Nadia's gymnastics center, she attended classes for four hours each morning and then had lunch and a nap. Afternoons were reserved for gymnastics training, and evenings were spent on homework. Despite her tiring schedule, Nadia was always eager and energetic. She often arrived early for her gymnastics workouts.

By the time she was eight, Nadia was competing in national meets. In 1969, she entered her first Junior National Championships, where she placed thirteenth. The next year, Nadia won the meet, and she went on to win it for the following

Early in her gymnastics career, Nadia began collecting dolls. Everywhere she went, Nadia bought a doll as a souvenir, and by the time she retired from competition she had collected over three hundred dolls from around the world.

two years as well. When she was nine, Nadia earned a place on Romania's national gymnastics team and started competing internationally.

After a string of national and international successes, Nadia prepared for her first Olympic Games in 1976. She and her team members traveled the world to participate in pre-Olympic meets. At the American Cup competition in New York City, Nadia amazed everyone when her performance on the vault earned her the first perfect 10 ever awarded in the United States. She also received a perfect score in the floor exercise and won the all-around championship.

But it was at the Olympics in Montreal where Nadia really shined. Nadia received seven perfect 10s and won gold medals in the balance beam, the uneven bars, and the all-around competition. She also won a bronze medal in the floor exercise and led the Romanians to a silver medal in the team competition.

Over the next few years, Nadia continued to compete. In 1980, she traveled to Moscow to participate in her second Olympics, where she won two gold medals and two silvers. Throughout her career, Nadia trained with coach Bela Karolyi, but in 1981 Bela defected to the United States. After a competition in the United States, Bela and his wife remained in America while the rest of the Romanian team flew home. Nadia stayed in Romania working on gymnastics but focused more and more on coaching instead of competing. At the 1984 Olympic Games in Los Angeles, Nadia accompanied the Romanian team as a coach rather than as a team member.

Five years later, Nadia also decided to defect to the United States. She began touring with an Olympic all-star show. Through her all-star performances, Nadia met U.S. gymnast and gold medalist Bart Conner, whom she married in 1996. Bart and Nadia started their own gymnastics school in Oklahoma, where they now live.

Through her brilliant performances, Nadia brought many new viewers and participants to gymnastics. She inspired countless girls to take part in the sport — girls like Olympic gold medalist Mary Lou Retton, who named Nadia as her role model. With her thrilling combination of strength and agility, Nadia will always be remembered as the first Olympic gymnast to score a perfect 10.

After returning home from the Olympics, Nadia was awarded a Hero of Socialist Labor medal from her government. It was the highest honor ever awarded in Romania.

Nadia admits that she occasionally indulges in her favorite foods: pizza and frozen Snickers bars. She also loves to watch her favorite soap opera, The Young and the Restless.

Sheryl Swoopes

1971– ✻ PROFESSIONAL BASKETBALL PLAYER ✻ UNITED STATES

She'll be a legend in women's basketball, but not just because of her play. She has a charisma that the crowd loves. You never doubt that she is a team player.

— Marsha Sharp, Sheryl's coach at Texas Tech

T he players on Texas Tech's women's basketball team were ecstatic — they had just won the 1993 college national championship! And they couldn't have done it without their star forward, Sheryl Swoopes. She led them to victory by scoring an amazing forty-seven points, setting a new record for most points scored in a national championship game — men's or women's. Sheryl's performance in the Final Four tournament also broke nine other records, including most points scored in the Final Four by a woman and most points scored in a women's tournament. Sometimes called the "female Michael Jordan," Sheryl's impact on women's basketball has been enormous. Along with many other great woman athletes, she has helped bring the sport long-overdue national popularity.

Sheryl Swoopes was born in Brownfield, Texas, on March 25, 1971. She grew up playing basketball with her brothers and their friends. In high school, she played on the girls' team and was named Texas Player of the Year when she was only a junior! In a state known for launching such star athletes as Babe Didrikson, this was an astounding feat. After high school, Sheryl played basketball for South Plains Junior College, where she set twenty-eight records and was named an All-American Player. She went on to Texas Tech, where her team won their conference both years Sheryl played there. They also won the national championship her senior year. Sheryl collected countless records and awards, including Player of the Year and Female Athlete of the Year.

After college, Sheryl wanted to continue playing basketball. Unfortunately, there weren't any professional women's basketball leagues in the United States yet, so Sheryl temporarily joined a team in Italy. But after playing only ten games there, she decided to return to Texas. She took a job as a bank teller and played pickup games at a local gym.

Sheryl and Eric were married on June 17, 1995. Her marriage wasn't the only exciting event for Sheryl that year. In May, she earned a place on the non-professional U.S. Women's National Team. She and her teammates toured Europe, Asia, and Australia to prepare for the 1996 Olympics. Sheryl and the U.S. Dream Team took

Playing with the guys at the gym could get pretty rough, especially when the other players became frustrated by Sheryl's awesome basketball abilities. Her boyfriend, Eric, would accompany her to the gym as a bodyguard to ensure that no one was a sore loser.

home the gold medal and won the hearts of thousands of new fans. When Nike introduced the popular "Air Swoopes" shoe, Sheryl became the first woman basketball player to have a shoe named after her. "Air Swoopes" sold out of stores immediately.

In 1997, Sheryl's dream finally came true. Thanks to the growing popularity of women's basketball and the demand from fans all over America, the Women's National Basketball Association was finally created. Sheryl was quickly signed to play for the Houston Comets. Finally, she could play professionally in the United States! She sat out much of the season, however, because she was pregnant with her first child. Just six weeks after the birth of her son, Swoopes returned to the court.

Along with other talented basketball players like Rebecca Lobo, Lisa Leslie, and Cynthia Cooper (the league's 1997 Most Valuable Player), Sheryl helped make the WNBA's first season a huge success. She even wrote a children's book about her life, called *Bounce Back*, to encourage girls to go for their dreams. She is a big supporter of the "Girls Movement" and a role model for girl athletes everywhere! But Sheryl's influence is best shown by a tribute from a girls' basketball team in Shallowater, Texas; in honor of their hero, these eight- and nine-year-old girls named themselves "The Swoopesters."

Sheryl named her son Jordan—after Michael Jordan, of course!

How Will You Rock the World?

"I will rock the world by being the best NBA player of all time. They will call me 'Air Monson,' and I will use my fame to be the best role model possible and to show girls that they can make a difference in the world."

Abby Monson, age 11

"I will rock the world by writing books for children with a moral in every story. I've already written one called 'The Big Idea.' Its moral is not to wait for people to help you acheive your goal—JUST DO IT!"

Jenna Vella, age 10

Wang Yani

1975– ✳ PAINTER ✳ CHINA

When you pick up a brush, don't ever ask anyone for help. Because the most wonderful thing about painting is being left alone with your own imagination. I do not paint to get praise from others, but to play a game of endless joy.
— Wang Yani

W ang Shiqiang couldn't believe his eyes — his painting was ruined! And the culprit? His two-and-a-half-year-old daughter, Yani. She had gotten into his oil paints while he was gone and used them to create her own "masterpiece" — right over her father's careful brush strokes. Wang Shiqiang was angry at first, but Yani explained, "Papa, I was helping you paint. I want to paint and paint." At that moment, Wang Shiqiang knew that his daughter's talent and desire would make her an amazing artist.

Wang Yani was born in Gongcheng, a small town in southern China. She expressed an interest in painting at a very young age, and her father, an art teacher and a painter, gave her the materials she needed. By the time she was three years old, Yani had already created paintings in the bold, dynamic style that would characterize all her work.

This young, inspired artist was only four years old when she held her first art exhibition in Shanghai. By age six, Yani had completed over four thousand paintings, and when she was eight, one of her paintings was made into a Chinese postage stamp.

Over the next few years, Yani's work was shown throughout Asia, Europe, and North America. Then, in 1989, she achieved something truly unheard of in the art world: at just fourteen years of age, she became the youngest person ever to have a one-person show at the famous Smithsonian Institution in Washington, D.C. Her exhibition was called "Yani: The Brush of Innocence."

Amazingly, Yani has never had any formal art training or painting classes. She paints just because she loves it. Her painting has been called "fresh" and "vigorous." Although her style is unique, she paints with traditional Chinese materials: brushes, inks, pigments, and special paper. Yani relies on her memory of real life experiences for inspiration, but she also uses her imagination to bring the paintings to life.

Before starting a painting, Yani tries to clear her mind. Often she listens to music while she works — Beethoven's Fifth Symphony is her favorite. After deciding what to paint, Yani begins to work, sweeping her brush smoothly across the paper.

Usually it takes Yani about thirty or forty minutes to complete a painting. When she's done, she marks the painting with her personal red seal, which, like a signature, identifies Yani as the artist.

Not everything is careful brushwork; Yani has even been known to pour ink directly onto the paper from her hands!

Yani's favorite subjects in her early paintings were animals, especially cats and monkeys. She paints these animals playing and being mischievous. Yani's later work portrays landscapes and people, and many of her paintings tell a story. She often uses her art as a way to communicate. Once, to show her mom that she was hungry, Yani painted a picture of a monkey eating fruit.

Yani devotes a lot of her time to painting. Even when she was in school, Yani managed to paint about three pictures a day. But she also made time for her other hobbies and interests, like singing, dancing, reading, writing, sports, and music. Yani's talent has brought her international acclaim, but it's her love for painting that inspires her to keep creating new work.

Vanessa-Mae Nicholson

1978– ✻ VIOLINIST ✻ SINGAPORE AND ENGLAND

*Violin playing is
a physical art with
great traditions
behind it. At its
best, it conveys the
qualities of beauty,
strength, and mys-
tique . . . So what I
like, I will want to
play. To me, music
. . . is for enjoying
and for playing.
This is the way of
the violin player.*
— Vanessa-Mae
Nicholson

The MTV video showed a young woman walking down the beach. She was dressed in a typical rock star outfit: tight pants and a sheer T-shirt. Just when viewers expected her to burst into a syrupy pop ballad, the magnetic young woman propped an electric violin on her shoulder and began rocking out to Bach's Toccata and Fugue in D Minor. Seventeen-year-old violinist Vanessa-Mae grinned at her own image on the screen. It sure wasn't what her classical fans would expect!

She was excited to break with tradition and transform herself into a pop artist, complete with the glamour and allure of other pop musicians. She wanted to attract a younger, hipper audience to her music. Never content to follow tradition, Vanessa-Mae found a way to combine pop and classical music to produce her own innovative style. It was a far cry from the classical orchestras and symphonies that she played in as a child, but teenage Vanessa-Mae was drawing in crowds of young new listeners with her unique musical sound.

Vanessa-Mae Vanakorn Nicholson was born in Singapore on October 27, 1978. The child of a Thai mother and a Chinese father, Vanessa-Mae began to study music at a very early age. When she was just four years old, she and her family moved to London, where she began taking violin lessons.

It was soon apparent that Vanessa-Mae had a special gift for the violin. When she was only ten, she played in her first concert with an orchestra, and she was touring internationally by the age of twelve. Vanessa-Mae also started recording her work, and by 1992, she had made three classical albums.

Today, Vanessa-Mae is known for more than just her classical music. She first started experimenting with an electric fiddle at age thirteen, and now her goal is "to do for the violin what Jimi Hendrix did for the guitar." With her pop-inspired performances on the electric violin, she has added a new dimension to traditional recordings. And if the success of her first pop album is any indication, Vanessa-Mae is off to a rocking start.

Released in 1995, *The Violin Player* debuted at No. 11 on Britain's Top 40 album charts. Vanessa-Mae's techno-infused version of Bach's Toccata and Fugue in D Minor hit the Top 20 *singles* charts as well. Vanessa-Mae's unique brand of music combines the electric violin with acoustic instruments and synthesized pop music, a style she calls "techno-acoustic fusion." The result is music with a wide appeal to both classical and pop fans.

With her crossover hits and modern, fashionable appearance, Vanessa-Mae is bringing something new to the violin. She is providing a fresh perspective for classical music, taking it in a new direction and broadening its appeal to include a younger generation: her own. For now, Vanessa-Mae plans to continue her work — making more music and literally rocking the world.

Cristen Powell

1979– ✳ DRAG RACER ✳ UNITED STATES

If the fans weren't out there watching, we wouldn't be racing. They wait for hours — even in the baking heat — just to watch us and get autographs. I get a lot of mail from kids who want to be drag racers, so it's kind of like I'm a role model for them. It's fun, and the fans make all the work worthwhile!
— Cristen Powell

Excited and a little nervous, Cristen stepped into her purple, fire-retardant racing suit. She pulled on a yellow helmet and strapped herself into her thirty-foot-long dragster. At just eighteen years old, she had already been drag racing for several years. Cristen shook off her anxiety. She had skipped her own prom for this race, and she wasn't going to mess it up now. She had just started competing in the Top Fuel category, the highest racing category there is, and was up against the fastest dragsters in the country. At the starting signal, Cristen pressed the accelerator. Her car jumped off the line and flew screaming down the quarter-mile straightaway. Seconds later, the race was over, and two parachutes shot out of the dragster's back end to slow it down.

Cristen couldn't believe it — she had won! She had raced against Top Fuel drivers, many of whom were twice her age, and had beaten them. This victory made her the youngest woman ever to win a Top Fuel race, and the second-youngest *person* to win (the youngest man was just one month younger than Cristen). She had sped down the quarter-mile track in 4.85 seconds, at a speed of 240 miles per hour! Cristen proved herself a tough competitor and a rising star on the racetrack.

Cristen Powell is the youngest of three sisters. She was born on March 22, 1979, in Philadelphia, Pennsylvania. She and her family moved to Oregon when she was two years old. In her teens, Cristen's attention turned to cars. Her father had been a drag racer, and as she learned to drive and bought her first car, a 1967 Camaro, fifteen-year-old Cristen's interest in the sport grew.

For her sixteenth birthday present, Cristen's dad enrolled her in a course at the Frank Hawley Drag Racing School in Florida to learn how to drive Super Comp dragsters, the most basic drag-racing cars. Cristen didn't even have her regular driver's license yet, but she earned her racing license after completing Frank Hawley's intense course.

As a young girl, Cristen loved horses. When she was thirteen, she won a national championship in dressage, a competition in which the rider takes her horse through difficult maneuvers and gaits.

A few months later, with her racing *and* regular license in hand, Cristen started racing competitively. After four national events and various divisionals, the motor in her Super Comp dragster blew up. Dragster-less, Cristen got a license upgrade to race in the next highest category, Federal Mogul dragsters (then called Top Alcohol cars), and leased a car. In her first national race for Top Alcohol cars, she was the number one qualifier—the youngest person ever to earn that rank.

The first car Cristen ever drove by herself was a dragster!

The next year, Cristen bought her own dragster and competed in thirty-two races. In addition to driving the car, she worked on its motor, with the help of her crew members. Cristen had an amazing year, qualifying first in six races. But her greatest achievement came at a race in Topeka, Kansas. Not only was she the number one qualifier, she also set a national record by hurtling down the quarter-mile track in just 5.44 seconds! Cristen's record-breaking performance caught the attention of veteran racer Jim Epler, who offered her the chance to drive one of his Top Fuel cars. Top Fuel is the highest racing category. Cristen would be racing with the fastest men and women in the country.

In 1997, she started racing Top Fuel dragsters. In her first race of the season, Cristen drove faster than she had ever driven before and proved she was a contender with the best drag racers in the country. Her first Top Fuel victory came in Englishtown, New Jersey, in May 1997. With this triumph, she became the youngest woman and the second-youngest person ever to win a national event.

Drag racers gain points for each competition they race in. The points are then totalled to determine the best overall dragsters. Although Cristen wasn't able to compete in every 1997 race, she expected to finish fourteenth that year out of the thirty or so best drag racers in America.

Cristen's incredible success during her first year shows that she is a talented driver. But she doesn't do it alone. She has a professional crew who makes sure her car is always in top condition, and her sponsor, Reebok, keeps her in firesuits. But most of all, Cristen appreciates her dedicated fans.

Cristen's race car

As a teenage girl, Cristen had to prove herself on the racing circuit. Women have been drag racing for about thirty years, but they are still a small minority in the sport. Most drivers are men. Many doubted that young Cristen could hold her own on the track. There are, however, a few women racers Cristen can look to as role models, including Cristen's hero, Shirley Muldowney. Shirley was the first woman ever to race Top Fuel dragsters and is still racing today.

Despite all the time she spends racing, Cristen finds time for a full freshman course load at college. She's a lot like other college freshmen and tries to keep her life as normal as possible. She is sometimes afraid that other students will treat her differently if they discover what she does in her spare time. After all, it's not every day you meet an eighteen-year-old girl who is a drag-racing star! When students do find out, they get over their shock quickly when they realize she is just a normal teenager.

Today, Cristen continues to find success and excitement on the racetrack. She plans to keep racing and working toward her college degree for the next few years. Like many young women, she's not sure what she wants to do for her entire life, but one thing's for sure: this gutsy, trailblazing girl will continue to show the world that girls can do anything!

How Will You Rock the World?

"I will rock the world by making horseback riding a well-known Olympic sport, like ice skating or gymnastics. The sport of

horseback riding doesn't receive the attention it deserves, and until it does, I'll keep spreading the horse-world word!"

Brianna York, age 13

Martina Hingis

[Martina] has a sophisticated game that is only going to get stronger. Her mom may be a great teacher, but this girl has a sense of the court that can't be taught. I have just seen the future of tennis . . . and it's thrilling.
— Bud Collins, sportswriter

Martina Hingis stood ready to return her opponent's next serve. She was losing the match and knew that if this ball got past her she would have no chance of winning. She focused on her opponent, the sweat stinging her eyes. It was the 1997 Wimbledon tournament, the most prestigious tennis tournament in the world. Sixteen-year-old Martina was playing against Jana Novotna in the singles final. So far Jana was winning the match, but Martina had kept her composure and concentration, and now she had a chance to pull ahead. If she could just win this point, Martina would be leading the second set and could possibly win the match.

She could see the ball rocketing toward her. With a smashing forehand shot, Martina slammed the ball back, right past Jana. All she could hear was the roar of the crowd. She had done it. Nothing could stop her now. Martina went on to win the match, becoming the youngest singles champion at Wimbledon in over one hundred years! As Martina proudly held up the championship plate, millions of Wimbledon viewers around the world celebrated the victory of tennis's newest star.

Martina Hingis was born on September 30, 1980, in Kosice, Czechoslovakia. She was given a sawed-off wooden tennis racket when she was only two years old. At age six, Martina won her first tournament, and by the time she was eight, she was beating players twice her age. In 1987,

Martina was named after tennis champion Martina Navratilova.

Martina moved to Switzerland with her mother and stepfather and continued playing tennis. By 1994, she was the number one junior player in the world. She turned pro that same year, at the age of fourteen!

Martina's first year as a pro was a difficult one. She was having trouble with her serve and was losing her motivation to compete. But when her mother gave her the choice between working seriously on her tennis game or going back to school full time, Martina wasted no time in choosing tennis.

From then on, Martina's game only improved. In 1996, she and her teammate won the doubles championship at Wimbledon, and she competed for the Swiss Olympic team. Her first singles championship at a Grand Slam event came in 1997, when she won the Australian Open. (The tennis Grand Slam events — the Australian Open, the French Open, Wimbledon, and the U.S. Open — are the four most prestigious events on the tour.) Martina's win in Australia made her the youngest player to win a Grand Slam singles event in over a century. After beating Monica Seles at the Lipton Championships in Miami, she was the youngest woman to be ranked number one in the world.

A couple of months before the 1997 French Open, Martina was injured while horseback riding, her favorite hobby. The injury required knee surgery, but Martina still managed to play in the French Open and even took second place. By July, she had fully recovered and became the youngest person to win at Wimbledon since 1887. That same season, she won her third Grand Slam title of the year at the U.S. Open.

Martina has awed the tennis world with her natural talent and her ability to choose the perfect shot for almost every situation. But her success requires hard work, practice, and sacrifice. On the tour, Martina is always accompanied by her mother, who is also her coach, and she usually practices for at least two and one-half hours a day. Because of tennis, Martina spends a lot of time traveling and is not usually in one place long enough to maintain a normal social life or to date. But she makes sure she has some time for fun. In her free time, she enjoys horseback riding, soccer, basketball, swimming, skiing, and rollerblading.

Martina is continuing her success in tennis. With her talent and dedication, there's no telling what she can achieve. Along with other rising teenage tennis stars like Anna Kournikova, Mirjana Lucic, and Venus Williams, Martina Hingis is ushering in a new generation of champions.

> *Although Martina doesn't get a traditional education on the road, she learns a lot from her traveling experiences. Martina can speak three languages — English, Czech, and German.*

How Will You Rock the World?

"I will rock the world by bringing peace to it. I plan to travel around the world talking about the importance of peace. I will study many languages so I can speak to people internationally. It shows that you care about the people's country when you take the time to learn their language."

Bassie Rotenberg, age 14

Notes

1. Plutarch, *Plutarch's Lives*, vol. 9, trans. Bernadotte Perrin (London: William Heinemann, 1968), 195-97.

2. W. W. Tarn, as quoted by Deborah G. Felder, *The 100 Most Influential Women of All Time: A Ranking Past and Present* (New York: Citadel Press, 1996), 303.

3. Sor Juana Inés de la Cruz, *A Sor Juana Anthology*, trans. Alan S. Trueblood (Cambridge, Mass.: Harvard University Press, 1988), 178.

4. Phillis Wheatley, *The Poems of Phillis Wheatley*, ed. Julian D. Mason, Jr. (Chapel Hill, N.C.: University of North Carolina Press, 1966), 89–90.

5. Reuben Gold Thwaites, ed., *Original Journals of the Lewis and Clark Expedition: 1804 – 1806*, vol. 2 (New York: Arno Press, 1969), 321.

6. George R. Stewart, *Ordeal by Hunger: The Story of the Donner Party* (Boston: Houghton Mifflin, 1960), 359.

7. Stewart, 359–60.

8. Giraud Chester, *Embattled Maiden: The Life of Anna Dickinson* (New York: G. P. Putnam's Sons, 1951), 93–94.

9. Emma Lazarus, *Poems of Emma Lazarus*, (Boston: Houghton Mifflin, 1899), 202-3.

10. Helen Keller, *The Story of My Life*, ed. John Albert Macy (New York: Doubleday, 1954), 21-22.

11. A. H. Wood and Elizabeth Wood Ellem, "Queen Salote Tupou III," in *Friendly Islands: A History of Tonga*, ed. Noel Rutherford (Melbourne, Australia: Oxford University Press, 1977), 209.

12. Andre Breton, "Frida Kahlo de Rivera," in *Frida Kahlo and Tina Modotti*, ed. Mark Francis (London: Whitechapel Art Gallery, 1982), 36.

13. Breton, 37.

14. Mary Leakey, *Disclosing the Past* (Garden City, N.Y.: Doubleday, 1984), 193.

15. Babe Didrikson Zaharias, *This Life I've Led: My Autobiography* (New York: A. S. Barnes, 1955), 88-89.

16. Zaharias, 76.

17. Indira Gandhi, *Letters to an American Friend: 1950 – 1984*, ed. Dorothy Norman (San Diego: Harcourt Brace Jovanovich, 1985), 178-79.

18. Anne Frank, *The Diary of a Young Girl: The Definitive Edition*, ed. Otto Frank and Mirjam Pressler, trans. Susan Massotty (New York: Doubleday, 1995), 1.

19. Frank, 281.

20. Tom Biracree, *Wilma Rudolph*, Women of Achievement Series (New York: Chelsea House, 1988), 107.

Recommended Reading
How to Find Out More About These
World-Rocking Girls!

Ambrose, Stephen E. *Undaunted Courage: Meriwether Lewis, Thomas Jefferson, and the Opening of the American West.* New York: Touchstone, 1996.

Ashby, Ruth, and Deborah Gore Ohrn, eds. *Herstory: Women Who Changed the World.* New York: Viking, 1995.

Baldwin, Louis. *Women of Strength: Biographies of 106 Who Have Excelled in Traditionally Male Fields.* Jefferson, N.C.: McFarland, 1996.

Barker-Benfield, G. J., and Catherine Clinton. *Portraits of American Women: From Settlement to the Present.* New York: St. Martin's Press, 1991.

Beckner, Chrisanne. *100 African-Americans Who Shaped American History.* San Francisco: Bluewood Books, 1995.

Biracree, Tom. *Wilma Rudolph.* Women of Achievement Series. New York: Chelsea House, 1988.

Charlot, Monica. *Victoria: The Young Queen.* Oxford: Basil Blackwell, 1991.

Daly, Jay. *Presenting S. E. Hinton.* New York: Dell, 1989.

Emboden, William. *Sarah Bernhardt.* New York: Macmillan, 1975.

Felder, Deborah G. *The 100 Most Influential Women of All Time: A Ranking Past and Present.* New York: Citadel Press, 1996.

Frank, Anne. *The Diary of a Young Girl: The Definitive Edition.* Edited by Otto Frank and Mirjam Pressler. Translated by Susan Massotty. New York: Doubleday, 1995.

Gupte, Pranay. *Mother India: A Political Biography of Indira Gandhi.* New York: Charles Scribner's Sons, 1992.

Hibbert, Christopher, ed. *Queen Victoria in Her Letters and Journals.* New York: Viking, 1985.

Keller, Helen. *The Story of My Life.* Edited by John Albert Macy. New York: Doubleday, 1954.

Krull, Kathleen. *Wilma Unlimited: How Wilma Rudolph Became the World's Fastest Woman.* New York: Harcourt Brace, 1996.

Leakey, Mary. *Disclosing the Past.* Garden City, N.Y.: Doubleday, 1984.

McGrayne, Sharon Bertsch. *Nobel Prize Women in Science: Their Lives, Struggles and Momentous Discoveries.* New York: Birch Lane Press, 1993.

Oliver, Paul. *Bessie Smith.* London: Cassell, 1959.

Rolka, Gail Meyer. *100 Women Who Shaped World History*. San Francisco: Bluewood Books, 1994.

Sebba, Anne. *Mother Teresa: Beyond the Image*. New York: Doubleday, 1997.

Shiels, Barbara. *Winners: Women and the Nobel Prize*. Minneapolis: Dillon, 1985.

Smith, Linda Irwin. *Women Who Write: From the Past and the Present to the Future*. Englewood Cliffs, N.J.: Julian Messner, 1989.

St. Aubyn, Giles. *Queen Victoria: A Portrait*. New York: Atheneum, 1991.

Stille, Darlene R. *Extraordinary Women of Medicine*. New York: Children's Press, 1997.

———. *Extraordinary Women Scientists*. Chicago: Children's Press, 1995.

Vare, Ethlie Ann, and Greg Ptacek. *Women Inventors and Their Discoveries*. Minneapolis: Oliver Press, 1993.

Vennema, Diane Stanley, and Peter Vennema. *Cleopatra*. New York: Morrow Junior Books, 1994.

Wepman, Denis. *Helen Keller*. American Women of Achievement Series. New York: Chelsea House, 1987.

Young, Bette Roth. *Emma Lazarus in Her World: Life and Letters*. Philadelphia: The Jewish Publication Society, 1995.

Zaharias, Babe Didrikson. *This Life I've Led: My Autobiography*. New York: A. S. Barnes, 1955.

Zhensun, Zheng, and Alice Low. *A Young Painter: The Life and Paintings of Wang Yani —China's Extraordinary Young Artist*. New York: Scholastic, 1991.

Additional Bibliography

Anderson, Kelli. "Rhymes with Hoops: Basketball Star Sheryl Swoopes." *Sports Illustrated*, 12 April 1993, p. 42.

Badran, Margot, and Miriam Cooke, eds. *Opening the Gates: A Century of Arab Feminist Writing*. Bloomington, Ind.: Indiana University Press, 1990.

Baring, Maurice. *Sarah Bernhardt*. Westport, Conn.: Greenwood Press, 1970.

Barnstone, Willis. *Six Masters of the Spanish Sonnet: Essays and Translations*. Carbondale, Ill.: Southern Illinois University Press, 1993.

Bernhardt, Sarah. *The Art of the Theatre*. New York: Dial Press, 1924.

Bhatia, Krishan. *Indira: A Biography of Prime Minister Gandhi*. New York: Praeger, 1974.

Brady, James. "She's Game, She's Set ... and a Match for Anyone: In Step with Martina Hingis." *Parade*, 17 August 1997, p. 12.

"The 50 Most Beautiful People in the World: Vanessa-Mae Nicholson." *People*, 6 May 1996, p. 150.

Garza, Hedda. *Frida Kahlo*. New York: Chelsea House, 1994.

Howard, Harold P. *Sacajawea*. Norman, Okla.: University of Oklahoma Press, 1971.

Jackson, Guida M. *Women Who Ruled*. Santa Barbara: ABC-CLIO, 1990.

Lerner, Gerda. *The Creation of Feminist Consciousness: From the Middle Ages to Eighteen-Seventy*. New York: Oxford University Press, 1993.

Marks, Geoffrey, and William K. Beatty. *Women in White: Their Role as Doctors through the Ages*. New York: Charles Scribner's Sons, 1972.

Miklowitz, Gloria D. *Nadia Comaneci*. New York: Grosset & Dunlap, 1977.

Neuls-Bates, Carol, ed. *Women in Music: An Anthology of Source Readings from the Middle Ages to the Present*. New York: Harper and Row, 1982.

Pearl, Daniel. "Voting Rites: Yemen Steers a Path Toward Democracy, with Some Surprises." *The Wall Street Journal*, 28 March 1997, p. A1.

Pendle, Karin, ed. *Women and Music: A History*. Bloomington, Ind.: Indiana University Press, 1991.

Pinckney, Eliza Lucas. *The Letterbook of Eliza Lucas Pinckney: 1739 – 1762*. Edited by Elise Pinckney. Chapel Hill, N.C.: University of North Carolina Press, 1972.

Rivera, Diego. "Frida Kahlo and Mexican Art." In *Frida Kahlo and Tina Modotti*. Edited by Mark Francis. London: Whitechapel Art Gallery, 1982.

Robinson, William H. *Phillis Wheatley in the Black American Beginnings*. Detroit: Broadside Press, 1975.

Schnabel, Ernst. *Anne Frank: A Portrait in Courage*. Translated by Richard and Clara Winston. New York: Harcourt, Brace, 1958.

Teresa, Mother. *Heart of Joy*. Ann Arbor: Servant Books, 1987.

Turner, Robyn Montana. *Frida Kahlo*. Boston: Little, Brown, 1993.

Vogel, Dan. *Emma Lazarus*. Boston: Twayne Publishers, 1980.

Wulf, Steve. "Love–15 at the Open." *Time*, 16 September 1996, p. 75.

"How Will You Rock the World?"

Write your dreams here:

Put your photo here:

Name:

Age:

Address:

Phone number (so we can call you if you win):

Cut out or photocopy this page and send it to:

Beyond Words Publishing, Inc.

20827 N.W. Cornell Road, Suite 500

Hillsboro, Oregon 97124-9808

You could be included in the next book,
More Girls Who Rocked the World!

WANT TO EARN YOUR OWN MONEY?
LEARN HOW TO START A BUSINESS!

Learn fun ways to earn $$$ as a
- babysitting broker
- dog walker
- mural painter

and many, many more!!!

Fifteen-year-old Daryl Bernstein started his first
business when he was just eight years old. Since then he's tried all 51 of the
kid businesses in this book. Daryl now runs his own multi-million-dollar
business and is ready to share his secrets with you!

"Dear Daryl,

When I got Better Than a Lemonade Stand, *I came up with a great business idea
and earned enough money to buy a laptop computer! I never knew it would only take
one summer to earn the money. Thanks for your help." —Brady, age 12*

150 pages, black & white cartoon art, $8.95 softcover

WELL, EXCUUUUSE US!!!
HERE ARE ALL THE EXCUSES YOU'LL EVER NEED!

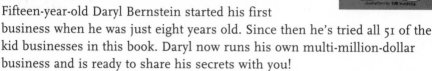

You'll get the best excuses for
- going to bed late
- not eating your vegetables
- not cleaning your room

and many, many more!!!

Mike and Zach are the excuse experts! At ages ten and
eleven, these best friends tested hundreds of excuses on family, friends, and
teachers in order to give you the best lines to get out of anything.

"Dear Mike and Zach,

*My whole class loves your book! I have an idea for excuses not to do your home-
work in the car: 'But Mom, it's homework, not carwork!'" —Blakeney, age 10*

96 pages, black & white cartoon art, $5.95 softcover

**For a free catalog or to order books,
call Beyond Words Publishing 1-800-284-9673**

118

HEY, GIRLS!!!
SPEAK OUT! BE HEARD!
BE CREATIVE! GO FOR YOUR DREAMS!

Discover how you can
- handle grouchy, just plain ornery adults
- pass notes in class without getting caught
- avoid life's most embarrassing moments
- unlock the writer inside you
and much, much more!!!

✸ A Scholastic Book Club Selection ✸

Girls Know Best celebrates your unique voices and wisdom. Thirty-eight girls, ages seven to fifteen, were picked to share their advice and activities with other girls. Everything you need to know . . . from the people who really know the answers—girls just like you!

160 pages, black & white collage art, $8.95 softcover

DO YOU HAVE A PSYCHIC PET?

Psychic Pets includes
- spooky stories of pets with psychic powers
- tests to find out if your pet is psychic
- tests to find out if you are psychic
- ways to increase your pet's psychic abilities
- astrology charts for your pet

✸ A Scholastic Book Club Selection ✸

Can your cat get out of the house even when all the doors are closed? Has your dog ever seen a ghost? Does your horse seem to read your mind? If you can answer yes to any of these questions, you might have a psychic pet!

"This amazing book is packed with incredible stories from all around the world, and there are fun psychic tests for you and your pet to do, too!" — Girl Talk magazine

124 pages, black & white art, $7.95 softcover

For a free catalog or to order books,
call Beyond Words Publishing 1-800-284-9673

ARE YOU A GODDESS IN THE MAKING?

Meet thirty-six goddesses, including
- Athena, the Greek goddess of wisdom
- Tara, the Tibetan goddess of mercy
- Pele, the Hawaiian goddess of fire

and many, many more!

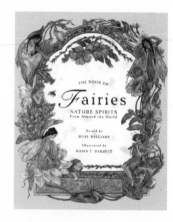

�֍ A Book-of-the-Month Club Selection �֍

Gorgeous illustrations and fascinating stories
will introduce you to goddesses from many dif-
ferent cultures. See the beauty, power, and wisdom of these goddesses and
learn how they are still honored in countries around the world.

64 pages, color illustrations, $17.95 hardcover

DO YOU BELIEVE?

Check out the *Fairy Flora Guide* that tells you
the special plants and flowers that fairies love.
You can even attract fairies to your house by
planting your own magical fairy garden!

�֍ A Book-of-the-Month Club Selection ✖

This book will introduce you to fairies, mer-
maids, pixies, and gnomes from around the
world. In this enchanting collection of stories
from France, China, England, India, Ireland,
Japan, and the Algonquian and Ojibwa tribes of America, fairies teach
humans the secrets of nature.

80 pages, color illustrations, $18.95 hardcover